HIBAKUSHA

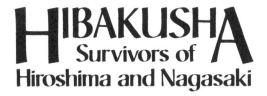

HIBAKUSHA
Survivors of
Hiroshima and Nagasaki

translated by
Gaynor Sekimori

with a foreword by
George Marshall

and an introduction by
Naomi Shohno

Kōsei Publishing Co. · *Tokyo*

The cover photograph shows the mushroom cloud formed when an atomic bomb exploded over Hiroshima at 8:15 A.M. on August 6, 1945. This photograph, formerly in the possession of the U.S. Armed Forces Institute of Pathology, is now the property of the Hiroshima Peace Culture Foundation and is used with the foundation's permission.

Editing, book design, typography, layout of photographs, and cover design by EDS Inc., Editorial & Design Services. Maps by Michio Kojima. The text of this book is set in a computer version of Baskerville with a computer version of Optima for display.

First English edition, 1986
Fifth printing, 2010

Published by Kōsei Publishing Co., Kōsei Building, 2-7-1 Wada, Suginami-ku, Tokyo 166. Copyright © 1984, 1985, 1986 by Kōsei Publishing Co.; all rights reserved. Printed in Japan.

ISBN 978-4-333-01204-6

Contents

Maps of Hiroshima and Nagasaki follow page 27
Photographs follow pages 56 and 120

Foreword

George Marshall
Minister, Unitarian Universalist Association

To go to Hiroshima today, after the building of a great new city, which like the phoenix of ancient folklore has risen from the ashes, is still a most moving experience. For me this occurred on a sunny, tranquil January day in 1982 when I visited Hiroshima for the first time. Since I was already in Japan, having concluded a visit to Osaka, the distance I traveled was not great, but in terms of its emotional impact, it was like traveling to the end of the earth. It was like a journey from the present to the most remote and terrifying primitive conditions of the dim past when humankind was still struggling to rise from the mire of its brutish beginnings. This was due not to the activities of the inhabitants of the city but to the unspeakable violence of the nuclear holocaust rained upon these people by my own countrymen.

Here I was, an educated American religious liberal, fairly well informed. As a young adult in the 1940s I participated as a loyal citizen in the war effort in behalf of my country. When the first atomic bomb in history was dropped on Hiroshima on August 6, 1945, I was totally unprepared for its effect and in consequence failed utterly to understand its implications.

That evening, being involved as an American noncombatant

7

serviceman on the eastern coast of the United States, I first heard of the bombing over the radio news program. However, it was not until January 1982 in Hiroshima that I comprehended in its full vividness what that catastrophe had meant in human suffering and the destruction of life. As I read the firsthand accounts of survivors of the Hiroshima and Nagasaki bombings included in this book, my mind was carried back to my own first awareness of the bomb, and what it meant to me. Even though I considered myself a human being highly sensitive to the suffering of others, I failed to comprehend the monstrous nature of that bomb. In part this failure was due to the secretive nature of the development of the bomb, so that only a select few in the United States understood the full implications of a nuclear explosion; and further, I, like most Americans, had been desensitized by the years of war.

Incendiary bombs, civilian warfare, destruction of cities, the bombing of London, of Dresden, of Berlin, of oh so many cities, had numbed the mind, so that one new bomb or wartime strike seemed so far away, so remote, and just one more of the dehumanizing aspects of war. This statement is not to excuse my insensitivity or that of any other American, but simply to try to express why it took me years to learn, and how it changed my life.

I have since returned to Hiroshima on August 6 for the great international observances that take place, with many thousands from many countries around the world coming on peace pilgrimage to bear witness to the universal cry of protest against nuclear warfare and hail the proclamation of the municipality of Hiroshima declaring itself forever a nuclear-free city. I have listened to the words and songs of thousands, seen again the monuments to peace, revisited the Peace Memorial Museum, walked the now-sacred paths thronging with peace pilgrims from around the world. But significant as such gatherings are, they lack the impact of that January day when I stood there alone, a solitary American, unsupported by thousands of like-minded Westerners supporting one another by a cacophony of sound and the excitement of group involvement.

That January, when standing alone in the park and later in the museum, a tall fair-skinned American beside my short dark-haired Japanese friend, I felt so alone, too easily identified as one of those who must have been the perpetrators of that treacherous crime against humanity. The aloneness and the silence created the condition for my penance that no thronging mass of humanity could ever create for me. In my mind's eye, I was suddenly "the American," the representative of my nation and my generation, and I suffered guilt by association. I was ashamed. I cried silently, inwardly. I wondered if the few visitors who were there looked at me and thought, "He is one of those who did this." That was what I thought, although, as I have said, I knew nothing of the development and building of such a bomb, or of the decision to use it. But in their eyes was I not "one of them"?

Why was I so upset? What caused me to feel like a partner in a crime in which I had not participated? Was it merely guilt by association? It was not that I was ignorant; I knew the figures of the total destruction of a city, of the two hundred thousand killed in the Hiroshima bombing. These probably suffered less than the thousands of anguished survivors, blinded, burned, their skin dripping from their bodies, their tongues swollen and parched from the lack of fresh water, their skin disfigured by horrible growths—the large, raised, unsightly, painful welts known as keloids. Then there was the internal damage to organs, bone marrow, flesh, genes, and blood cells, so that the diseases of nuclear exposure were passed on to the following generation, if indeed it was possible to conceive progeny. One could read these facts, but in human terms something more graphic, more explicit, brought out for me the full force of what they meant to people. This I discovered when alone in Hiroshima on that January day.

One needed time to meditate as one walked slowly through the Peace Memorial Museum, earphone in place, listening to the cassette recorder that told specifically what each display represented. With glistening eyes I followed the instructions of the museum narrator as I observed, and listened, and had my own private thoughts. In my mind I was carried back to my own ignorance of the events of that day when, newly married, I enjoyed my wife's good company as the radio mechanically reported the day's wartime events of August 6. As I have indicated, we were already inured to the extravagant claims of new military equipment bringing military superiority as more efficient ways of annihilating "the enemy" were extolled, so that it took another twelve or twenty hours for me to fully appreciate the total destruction of a city by a single bomb. With the publication of photographs the next day, one realized that a terrible swift form of destructive power had been unleashed and that the nature of warfare was now more hideous than ever, no longer a matter to bring rejoicing.

Then came the bragging about how this had been the best-kept secret of the war effort; how there had been a mobilization of scientists, industrialists, and engineers in scattered centers across the continent to work on the various components of this project, so that only a tiny command center knew what the result would be. Thus the truth was hidden not only from the public but from many of the bomb's creators so that no conscientious objection could be raised by those in a position to expose the hideous nature of the project.

Those who have been to Hiroshima know that the Peace Memorial Museum stands at the entrance to Peace Memorial Park, facing the famed skeletal dome of the ruins of the Industrial Promotion Hall. As one walks slowly down the path along the waterway, one sees many memorials erected not only by the Japanese people but by the sorrowing people of many countries around the world. People everywhere wish to atone for some of the damage, to assume a portion of the pain and sorrow felt by the survivors and their families, joining in what Dr. Albert Schweitzer called "the fellowship of those who bear the mark of pain." The whole world has come to bear that burden of pain for those who lived here on that fateful day. Here also are the Flame of Peace, the Peace Tower, the Bell of Peace, and the stone cenotaph containing a register of the bomb's victims. The souls of 120,000 victims are said to be enshrined in the memorial mound.

Hiroshima was declared a Peace City on August 6, 1949, four years to the day after the atomic blast. To the right of the museum stands Peace Memorial Hall. On that January day they were showing newly released documentary films of the explosion and, what was even worse, the anguish and pain of the many victims who went to the temporary medical facilities for aid. I was witness to a scene later reported in the press but at the time explained to me by my Japanese companion, who understood, as I did not, what we saw: a person in the scant audience began to cry out and ran down front, pointing to the hospital scene, crying out that one victim covered with keloids and obviously in great pain was his brother, whose fate he had been seeking these many years. Thus the continuing reality of the travail was once again impressed upon my mind.

How can one describe the suffering of the people in the pictures we saw? No one close to the great fireball blast survived, but those at some distance did, some for a brief nightmare of living hell and others for many years, as is witnessed in the following pages, a nightmarish hell that shall haunt them all the days of their lives. They must have coped with terrible adversities, including discrimination against their basic human rights to marriage, to a normal family life, to employment, to peaceful sleep with happy dreams, and including the loss of loved ones whose lives should not have been so hideously taken from them. Worse still may have been the continuing fear, if not the reality, of radiation sickness. Cancer and hepatitis are but examples of the problems they had to cope with or at least fear. As one survivor writes in her account, "The issue of the atomic bomb does not belong to history; it affects us here and now." Not only will it affect them as long as they live, they worry that after death radiation sickness may affect their descendants, haunting them throughout their lives.

How gross that some Americans have gloried in this affair! I think of the November 1946 "atomic bomb cake" festivity at the Army War College Officers Club, photographed with two admirals and a wife cutting the cake, which led Americans everywhere to protest against the obscenity of that event (see

Time, November 18, 1946, for an account). Again, I think of the offensive display at an air show in Harlingen, Texas, in October 1976, when retired Air Force Brigadier General Paul W. Tibbets, the pilot of the *Enola Gay,* reenacted the dropping of the bomb by dropping a ''demonstration bomb'' that erupted into a mushroom-shaped cloud. This event was commemorated by Sadako Kurihara, a Japanese poet and survivor of Hiroshima, who wrote a long poem that reads in part:

> Across the sea
> Hiroshima was repeated as an attraction at an air show;
> A mushroom cloud was made to soar up
> High into Texas' autumn sky.
> The spectators
> Were not burned by a flash
> Were not blanketed by the ashes of death
> Were not soaked by a tarry black rain.
> . . . .
> ''We shall not repeat the mistake.''
> So we vowed.
> But it is you who must vow, America—
> You who possess the bombs
> To burn Hiroshima a hundred million times over.
> Do not perish at your own hands.

Protests against such insensitive and callous displays by the general and admirals came not from Japan alone but also from across the American continent, from press, media, church groups, college campuses, and what we call the grass-roots voice of America, which unfortunately is not always the voice of national policy but which will become so in time as public sentiment grows.

The first bomb was so successful that it is difficult to think of any justification for dropping a second bomb a few days later on Nagasaki. If any excuse could be offered that the first bomb was more destructive and inhumane than had been anticipated, that argument could not be used thereafter. There could be no moral, or even military, justification for a second bomb. This is important, because many justifications were offered the American people for the use of the first bomb. It was said that the Nazis were feverishly at work seeking to split the atom and create a nuclear device, and that it was necessary that we do so before them; it was said that such a demonstration of a nuclear bomb would end the war in Japan and save the hundreds of thousands of lives that would be sacrificed in an invasion, although the incendiary bombs already dropped on Tokyo tended to make it appear that an invasion would not be necessary and that the war was all but over, since sober minds were already preparing to save the great cities of Japan from such carnage.

Part of the horror must be that a highly civilized nation possessing deep-seated ideals and holding values of human decency was capable of perpetrating this heinous crime. War reduces the sensitivities of people to the primitive level and pulls a shroud over the moral conscience of nations. Why then did we—the United States government—do it? Could it be that the military had a new device that it had to use? After the First World War, Field Marshal Douglas Haig, one of the great British field commanders, wrote in his memoirs that when he was a young man he believed that the way to prevent war was to prepare for war but now saw that if you prepare for war, you get war. The chronicler of the conquest of Mount Everest, James Uhlman, wrote that "men must climb it because it is there." In like manner, was there any reason for the use of this bomb other than that "it was there"? Like small children, the generals could not keep their hands off it once it was in their possession. If there is any other reason to justify the nuclear freeze movement or the disarmament discussions, it is to be found in this fact.

Is it too much to hope that Japan, as the only country that has felt the full fury of the atomic blast, might take the moral leadership in the world to outlaw the use of nuclear weapons? As citizens of the only unarmed major power in the world today, its people have the opportunity to throw their nation's considerable moral, economic, and strategic weight behind greater efforts for total disarmament. By religious tradition, economic strength, and the victimization of total war, Japan holds a unique position in the world, which perhaps it does not itself recognize, to take such world leadership for peace. Japan certainly should not bow to shortsighted calls for its rearmament, from whatever quarter they may come. The many thousands of world citizens who come to Hiroshima on August 6, and the equally potent observances in almost every major city of the world on that date, are but indications of the power of the Japanese witness for which the world yearns.

We in the West are heartened by the leadership already taken by Japanese groups and people. I think of the millions of names collected on a petition for disarmament gathered by members of the Japan-based lay Buddhist organization Rissho Kosei-kai and presented to the second Special Session of the United Nations General Assembly on Disarmament in New York in June 1982. I think of the establishment of the Niwano Peace Prize to honor peace activists for their contributions. I think of the Peace Tower built by the Reverend Toshio Miyake outside his church in Osaka, the Konko-kyo Church of Izuo. It is reported that he prays for peace every day that he is in the city and that many others from around the world, on visiting Osaka, also pray there for peace.

Demonstrations for peace are held in many lands today, and this is good, but there is a quality to Japanese concern too often absent elsewhere, and that is the spiritual and religious dimension as opposed to the political, which we see so often in the European protests against deployment of nuclear weapons. Perhaps this is part of the Japanese tradition, but it contains the moral leadership needed in the contemporary world. I have written elsewhere about the possibility of each person's becoming a Center for World Peace, by which I mean that each one of us can dedicate himself or herself to taking every possible step to advance the cause of peace and to create an inner attitude—a spiritual attitude—for peace. We need to be activists for peace, not merely spokespeople for peace.

I suggest that we need to inculcate the attitude toward peace found in the prayer for peace delivered in February 1981 in Hiroshima by Pope John Paul II:

"Hear my voice, for it is the voice of the victims of all wars and violence among individuals and nations;

"Hear my voice, for it is the voice of all children who suffer and will suffer when people put their faith in weapons and war;

"Hear my voice when I beg you to instill into the hearts of all human beings the wisdom of peace, the strength of justice and the joy of fellowship;

"Hear my voice, for I speak for the multitudes in every country and in every period of history who do not want war and are ready to walk the road of peace;

"Hear my voice and grant insight and strength so that we may always respond to hatred with love, to injustice with total dedication to justice, to need with the sharing of self, to war with peace.

"O God, hear my voice and grant unto the world *your everlasting peace.*"

Introduction

Naomi Shohno
Professor, Hiroshima Jogakuin College

On the morning of August 6, 1945, an atomic bomb rent the sky above Hiroshima and transformed the city into a hell on earth. A second bomb, dropped three days later on Nagasaki, recreated the hell that Hiroshima had become.

At the time I was a first-year student of physics in the Faculty of Science of Kyushu University in Fukuoka. On August 9 I returned to my home in Hiroshima to find out if my parents were safe and saw for myself the frightful destruction that had been wreaked on the city. Happily, my parents had survived, but many of my neighbors, friends, acquaintances, and teachers had been killed. That experience exerted a crucial influence on my life and thinking; I became a researcher in nuclear physics after graduation from university, and I also began to think about the sin Japan had committed in perpetrating a war of aggression, the great social responsibility of scientists in this nuclear age, and my own mission to work for the abolition of nuclear weapons.

The experiences of the twenty-five people recorded in this book will, I am sure, jolt the reader's mind. When I read accounts of the experiences of *hibakusha,* survivors of the atomic bomb, the wretchedness that I saw on August 9 looms up before me, and I suffer again. Because the experience of Hiroshima and Nagasaki was unique in the million years of human history, we have no more valuable source than the words of those who were there. If we are to surmount the crisis of the nuclear age, we must begin by chiseling deep into our minds the cruel events that the survivors have put into words for us.

At the same time, in order to fathom the reality of nuclear weapons, that evil force spawned by modern science, it is important that we understand them in scientific terms. If we read the experiences of the survivors with this scientific knowledge in mind, the meaning of the monstrous events of Hiroshima and Nagasaki and the consequences of nuclear war will be plain to us. It is from this viewpoint that I present some scientific data concerning the damage done at Hiroshima and Nagasaki, which I have studied as a theoretical physicist. (The data are taken from my book *The Legacy of Hiroshima: Its Past, Our Future,* Tokyo, Kosei Publishing Co., 1986.)

THE REALITY OF THE ATOMIC BOMB

Energy   The uranium bomb dropped on Hiroshima exploded about 580 meters above the central part of the city. The Nagasaki bomb, of the plutonium type, exploded about 500 meters above the Urakami basin in the northwestern part of the city. It is estimated that the energy produced by the Hiroshima bomb was equivalent to 15 kilotons of TNT and that of the Nagasaki bomb to 21 kilotons of TNT.

The figures of 15 and 21 kilotons roll off our tongues easily enough but give us no inkling of the extraordinary energy they represent in terms of traditional firepower. A B-29, the biggest bomber the United States had at the time, was able to carry 5 metric tons of bombs. Three thousand B-29s would have been necessary to carry the amount of TNT equivalent to the atomic bomb dropped on Hiroshima. For Nagasaki, 4,200 B-29s would have been required. Even supposing that there were that many B-29s in existence, it would have been impossible to deploy them all on one raid. In fact, there were only about 1,000 B-29s at the time. Even in these terms, the advent of the atomic bomb signaled a complete change from traditional weapons.

Blast and thermal rays   From data accumulated during postwar nuclear tests, we know that a 20-kiloton A-bomb, exploded at an altitude of 600 meters, produces a fireball with a temperature of several million degrees centigrade, or Celsius, and an atmospheric pressure of several hundred thousand bars. The fireball expands rapidly, reaching its maximum radius of 230 meters one second after the explosion. The fireball maintains its brightness for approximately ten seconds. The temperature of the fireball falls from 7,000 degrees centigrade 0.1 second after ex-

Table 1. Damage by Blast

Degree of damage	Distance from hypocenter (km)		Blast over-pressure (t/m^2)	Wind velocity (m/s)
	Hiroshima	Nagasaki		
Total destruction of almost all buildings and other structures	0.9	1.1	8.4	150
Total destruction of light steel-frame buildings and of wooden structures	1.6	1.8	3.5	74
Partial destruction of wooden structures	2.8	3.1	1.4	34
Light damage to buildings, shattered windowpanes	4.3	4.8	0.7	18

Note: For comparative purposes, overpressure of 1 to 10 metric tons per square meter is considered to destroy most artificial structures. The maximum wind velocity of a typhoon is approximately 80 meters per second.

plosion to 1,500 degrees centigrade three seconds later. Particularly strong thermal rays are emitted during these first three seconds. At the hypocenter, the point on the ground directly below the burst point, the energy of the thermal rays reaches 160 calories per square centimeter, so that the ground temperature rises to between 3,000 and 4,000 degrees centigrade. (By comparison, the melting point of iron is 1,550 degrees centigrade.)

The atmospheric pressure produced at the burst point rapidly expands the surrounding air and creates a tremendously strong blast. A shock wave of supersonic velocity (the speed of sound is 340 meters per second) travels about 740 meters from the burst point in the first second and about 11 kilometers in thirty seconds, after which it weakens rapidly. The shock wave is followed

Table 2. Damage by Thermal Rays

Degree of damage	Distance from hypocenter (km)		Thermal energy (cal/cm^2)
	Hiroshima	Nagasaki	
Almost everything catches fire; fatal burns	1.3	1.6	15.0
Conflagration occurs; third-degree burns	2.0	2.3	7.3
Fires occur; second-degree burns	2.5	2.9	4.5
Wood and black clothing scorch	3.0	3.5	3.0
First-degree burns	3.5	4.0	2.3

Note: First-degree burn: red burn; second-degree burn: white and spotted coagulation; third-degree burn: white and uniform coagulation. Third-degree burns over 25% of the body and second-degree burns over 30% of the body will cause death if untreated. The thermal energy of the sun's rays reaching the ground in Japan at midday in August over a three-second period (the period of intense emission of thermal rays by the atomic bomb) is 0.06 cal/cm^2.

by a wind of subsonic velocity. These two effects are responsible
for the destructive power of the blast. At the hypocenter the
blast overpressure (the amount by which the shock wave's pressure exceeds the natural atmospheric pressure) and wind velocity
reach 36 metric tons per square meter and 440 meters per second, respectively.

Generally speaking, when an atomic or a hydrogen bomb ex-
plodes in the air, about 50 percent of the total energy generated
is released in the form of blast, 35 percent in thermal rays, and
15 percent in radiation. The effects of blast and thermal rays
caused by the 15-kiloton Hiroshima bomb and the 21-kiloton
Nagasaki bomb are shown in Tables 1 and 2. The combined effects of blast, thermal rays, and fire virtually obliterated the area
within about two kilometers of the hypocenter in Hiroshima and
within about two and a half kilometers in Nagasaki.

Initial radiation   Victims of the bombing in both Hiroshima and
Nagasaki were unknowingly exposed to radiation, since this was
the first time that a military weapon had produced radiation.
The injuries caused by blast, thermal rays, and fire were visible;
those caused by radiation were not.

Initial radiation, the large amount of gamma rays and neutrons emitted from the fireball in the first minute after the explosion of a nuclear weapon, accounts for roughly 5 percent of the
total energy of the explosion. There are still some unresolved
questions in regard to the amount of initial radiation released in
the Hiroshima and Nagasaki explosions, but the numerical values in Table 3 provide food for thought.

In considering the influence of initial radiation on the human
body, we can regard the simple sum of the gamma-ray dose and
the neutron dose as the primary criterion. Thus we can see that
strong radiation was emitted within two kilometers of the hypocenter. People exposed to a "half-lethal dose" of 450 rads (the
rad, or "radiation absorbed dose," is the unit measuring the
amount of radiation absorbed in tissue), of whom 50 percent
died, were at a distance of one kilometer from the hypocenter in
Hiroshima and 1.15 kilometers in Nagasaki.

Residual radiation Another type of radiation is known as residual radiation, which affects the human body for a long period following the first minute after the explosion. Residual radiation accounts for approximately 10 percent of the total energy of the explosion.

Residual radiation consists of alpha, beta, and gamma rays, which are emitted from two types of residual radioactivity: induced radioactivity and fallout radioactivity. Induced radioactivity is caused by the collision and reaction with the soil and artificial structures of neutrons emitted in initial radiation. The greatest amount of induced radioactivity is produced at the hypocenter, where the number of neutrons is greatest. This type of radioactivity has a comparatively short life. Most fallout radioactivity consists of the nuclear-fission products of uranium or plutonium and is precipitated by rain, wind, or natural fall. This kind of radioactivity has a very long life.

Table 3. Initial Radiation Dose (T65D), in Rads

Distance from hypo-center (km)	Hiroshima		Nagasaki	
	Gamma rays	Neutrons	Gamma rays	Neutrons
0	10,300	14,100	25,100	3,900
0.5	2,790	3,150	7,090	703
1.0	255	191	888	35.9
1.5	21.6	10.1	119	1.7
2.0	1.9	0.5	17.8	0.1

Note: T65D (tentative 1965 dose) refers to the estimates of the initial radiation dose in relation to the radiation effects in Hiroshima and Nagasaki made in 1965 by the Oak Ridge National Laboratory in the United States. The estimates include an allowable margin of plus or minus 15% for Hiroshima and of plus or minus 10% for Nagasaki. Rad (radiation absorbed dose) is the unit of measure of the dose of radiation absorbed in tissue itself. The amount of radiation that the human body absorbs from natural sources is about 0.1 rad per year. The maximum dose that an ordinary individual may safely receive, aside from natural or medical radiation, has been set at 0.5 rad per year.

These two kinds of residual radioactivity, which affected both those in the city at the time of the explosion and those who entered the city later, caused damage in the following ways:

1. Those who were within one kilometer of the hypocenter in Hiroshima and within 0.8 kilometer of the hypocenter in Nagasaki in the first one hundred hours (four days) after the explosion were potentially exposed to a considerable amount of gamma rays from the induced radioactivity in the soil. The maximum dose of radiation was about 120 rads in Hiroshima and about 50 rads in Nagasaki. There would also have been the influence of the induced radioactivity in artificial structures, but it is difficult to determine the exact amount.

2. In the northwestern part of Hiroshima, where rain fell over a wide area after the explosion, and in the Nishiyama district in the eastern part of Nagasaki, there was a considerable amount of fallout. The highest dose of gamma rays received externally from fallout was about 20 rads in Hiroshima and about 200 rads in Nagasaki in the first month after the explosion. Those who entered the Nishiyama district of Nagasaki even one month after the explosion could have been exposed to up to 70 rads.

3. Those who ingested water or food contaminated by residual radioactivity or who inhaled a large amount of dust while handling the dead or while clearing up wreckage could have received a significant dose of internal radiation due to all the alpha, beta, and gamma rays.

Acute injuries   "Atomic bomb disease" is a general term for the diseases caused by blast, thermal rays, and radiation. A group of symptoms that appeared within four months of the explosion are called "acute injuries." In addition to external wounds and burns, these symptoms include general malaise, susceptibility to fatigue, headaches, nausea, vomiting, anorexia (loss of appetite), diarrhea, fever, oral and pharyngeal lesions, leukopenia (abnormally low white blood cell count), anemia, hemorrhagic diathesis (bloody discharges), and epilation (loss of hair). Injuries particularly connected with radiation include epilation, hemorrhagic diathesis, oral and pharyngeal lesions, and leukopenia.

Most of those who received serious injuries died within four months of the bombing. The symptoms of those who escaped death appeared to clear up after four months, and both doctors and victims thought that the bomb's effects had ended.

Aftereffects   However, some time after acute injuries subsided, protuberant scars known as keloids began to develop over wounds and burns. Their incidence peaked in 1946–47 and occurred most commonly among victims in their teens.

In 1947 cataracts caused by radiation began to occur, their incidence highest among survivors exposed within 1.6 kilometers of the hypocenter in Hiroshima and within 1.8 kilometers of the hypocenter in Nagasaki.

Leukemia due to radiation began to occur in 1947. Its incidence was highest in the 1950–54 period and decreased thereafter. Until 1978 the average incidence per year for survivors who had been exposed to more than 100 rads of radiation was 60 per 100,000 population in Hiroshima and 28 per 100,000 population in Nagasaki. These figures far exceed the national yearly average of 4 per 100,000 population.

The incidence of other forms of cancer among survivors began to become significant around 1960. By around 1970, the forms definitely attributed to radiation included thyroid, breast, and lung cancer. Moreover, several surveys made by 1980 proved that the death rate from cancer of the salivary glands, esophagus, stomach, colon, urinary tract, and bone marrow among those irradiated by more than 200 rads was definitely higher than the national average.

There is at present no proof of genetic effects due to radiation in the children of those who were exposed. This may be attributed in part to the early death of victims who were exposed to high amounts of radiation and to the miscarriage or stillbirth of malformed babies. At any rate, perhaps it is some small consolation to know that no harmful genetic effects have yet been confirmed, though some babies born to women exposed to radiation during pregnancy suffered from microcephaly.

Number of deaths   Even today there are no accurate figures for
the numbers who died in the atomic bombings. The chief reason
is that public offices were obliterated and most of their records
destroyed. Furthermore, the number of military personnel in
Hiroshima at the time is unknown, since the records were disposed of in the turmoil immediately after the war. These facts
show clearly the frightfulness of the bombs' destruction and the
misery of war.

Nevertheless, the following figures are considered reasonably
accurate: in Hiroshima, 130,000 to 140,000 died of acute injuries within the first four months after the explosion, out of a
population of 350,000; in Nagasaki, 60,000 to 70,000 died within the first four months, out of a population of 270,000. According to a survey in Hiroshima, 74 percent of those who died in
the first four months died the day of the bombing, and 89 percent died within two weeks. Due to aftereffects of the bombings,
the death rate of victims since 1946 has been clearly higher than
the national average, but no accurate figures are available.

Living in Japan today are about 237,000 survivors who experienced the bombings directly, 124,000 who were affected by
residual radiation, and 6,000 who were exposed in utero. Of
these survivors, about 4,000 are Koreans, and about 75 percent
currently live in the prefectures of Hiroshima and Nagasaki.

The suffering of the hibakusha   Survivors who are afflicted with
atomic bomb disease obviously undergo mental as well as
physical suffering. But *all* survivors live in the constant fear that
any sickness may turn out to be atomic bomb disease. Though
there is no scientific basis for such an assumption, survivors cannot help feeling that this disease is lurking within them. And
there is as yet no specific treatment for atomic bomb disease.
Whenever survivors fall ill, they are haunted by the fear of
death.

Memories of the shocking sights and fears of that time remain
deeply embedded in survivors' minds. Whenever they fall ill,
whenever they read or hear reports of nuclear weapons and tests,
whenever war or death is mentioned, the survivors recall the

events of 1945 as if they had occurred but yesterday and suffer deeply. Another keenly felt source of distress is the fact that despite Japan's postwar economic growth and social development, the government has not extended adequate aid to the surviving victims of the atomic bomb. The hardships entailed in rebuilding lives after Hiroshima and Nagasaki were very different from the difficulties people experienced as a result of other kinds of catastrophes.

Furthermore, survivors are made to feel that their experience has been meaningless when their pleas for the abolition of nuclear weapons go unheeded amid the arms race and its recurring nuclear tests. Many feel alienated from society, believing that their suffering can only be understood by other survivors. Many others, however, believe that they must reach out and devote their lives to building a world at peace, free from the menace of nuclear war.

THE MEANING OF HIROSHIMA AND NAGASAKI

The nuclear weapons in existence today are said to be equivalent to 20,000 megatons of TNT, or 1.33 million bombs of the kind exploded over Hiroshima. If these weapons were distributed over the 135 million square kilometers of the earth excluding Antarctica, there would be one Hiroshima-type bomb every 100 square kilometers (the approximate size of Hiroshima when it was bombed). Even thinking of these figures makes us realize that humankind could face extinction if there were total nuclear war.

Seen from space, the earth is a beautiful sphere. But the fate of all who live on "Spaceship Earth" is inextricably linked with death because of the development of nuclear weapons. If we cannot bring about the abolition of these weapons, we will be powerless to solve the other great problems facing us: the destruction of the environment, the inequalities between North and South, controls on science and technology. The abolition of nuclear weapons is the touchstone of basic human values.

The meaning of Hiroshima and Nagasaki lies in our asking ourselves what we can and should do in the face of this critical problem.

First, we must never forget that nuclear weapons are of an inhumanity beyond description. For this reason we must know exactly what nuclear weapons and nuclear war are like and must tell as many people as possible about the experiences of the *hibakusha*.

Second, to survive the nuclear age we must adopt a completely new way of thinking. It is vital that the United States and the Soviet Union, which possess close to 95 percent of the world's nuclear weapons, realize their deep responsibility toward the human race and resolve the hostility and distrust that lie between them. Both countries must develop the positive attitude that capitalism and communism can coexist. At the same time, we must all reconsider the old belief that peace can be imposed by a single power or a single principle. We who live at the most critical time in the history of humankind are being pressed to reexamine the values of the past and to create a new value system.

Also necessary is a radical change in the way we view nation-states. We can no longer tolerate old ways of thinking that excuse war, brutality, and the development of new weapons for the sake of the nation. Such ideas must be abandoned. When individuals become members of a large organization, they tend to become illogical and inhumane without the least compunction. We must discard absolute values regarding the nation, revise our ethical principles, and build a new world order.

At the same time, we must transmit to future generations the basic ethics that humankind has fostered over the ages, such as consideration for others and self-control. While individuals may harbor evil in their minds, they also possess a sense of goodness and justice that prompts them to control and improve themselves so that all may live together in a humane manner. We must trust this humaneness, join hands while admitting differences in thought, beliefs, and social systems, and create a public mood that demands abolition of the nuclear weapons that threaten our world. With such cooperation, we will be able to go on to create a new, truly human world order.

On the cenotaph to the victims of the atomic bomb in Peace Memorial Park in Hiroshima is inscribed a pledge that I consider to epitomize the meaning of Hiroshima and Nagasaki: "Let all souls here rest in peace; for we shall not repeat the evil." These words, rising above bitterness toward those who dropped the bomb, express concern for the future of the entire human race. This loving concern is the true spirit of Hiroshima and Nagasaki.

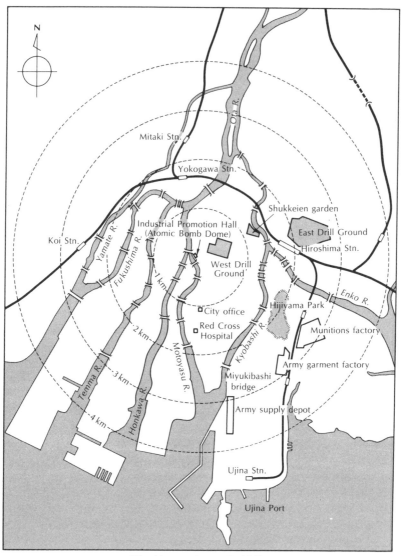

Hiroshima on August 6, 1945

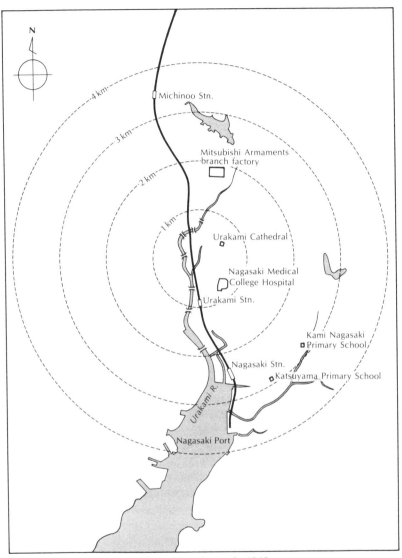

N

4 km
3 km
2 km
1 km

Michinoo Stn.

Mitsubishi Armaments
branch factory

Urakami Cathedral

Nagasaki Medical
College Hospital

Urakami Stn.

Kami Nagasaki
Primary School

Nagasaki Stn.

Katsuyama Primary School

Urakami R.

Nagasaki Port

Nagasaki on August 9, 1945

HIBAKUSHA

Hiroshima Flash

Kosaku Okabe

"No trains from here on. All passengers please alight." Following the conductor's instructions, we all got out at Koi Station, on the outskirts of Hiroshima. No one had the slightest idea what it was all about. On that hot, bright summer day my uniform was soaked with sweat.

There was talk going around that some hours previously a large bomb had been dropped on Hiroshima. I talked with a superior officer and decided to walk on into Hiroshima. In the immediate vicinity the damage did not appear too serious: roofs tilted slightly, broken or displaced roof tiles. However, as I walked on I realized why the train could go no farther. The lines were twisted like strings of jelly, and the ties, torn from their beds, lay upside down.

At that time I was so desensitized by the war that I was living each day with the sole purpose of killing more and more people. My feelings were so paralyzed that I was more like a demon than a human being. I hardly thought about what I saw, but just kept on walking.

As I approached the first river and looked down at the riverbed, I saw two large cows lying together with their horns sunk in the sand, and nearby, three pigs. In front of me, smoke still

33

overhung the city, and there was increasing confusion as the people leaving the city met those trying to enter it. I began to come across people with tattered clothing and injuries of a kind I had never seen before.

By now the area around me was a burned-out wasteland, with no houses standing. It was when I crossed what I think was the Ota River, though, that I really seemed to step into hell. In places the railing of the bridge had been completely blown away. Dead bodies lay where they had fallen. The great cherry trees that had lined the embankment were stripped of their branches, which were now hanging down in shreds from the trunks.

Looking downstream to the river mouth, I saw strange black shapes almost obliterating the sparkling sandbars. At that time people made turpentine from pine roots, and I assumed that these shapes were piles of roots. However, as I drew nearer I realized that in reality they were dead bodies, possibly deposited there by the river. Many strong impressions from that day are still with me, but this remains one of the most vivid. Perhaps the people had fled to the sandbar to escape the fierce heat of the flames as their houses burned around them. Perhaps they had run here, forcing their injured bodies along, their throats parched. There was a flurry of footprints leading to the water's edge. Farther on, in the water, floated countless bodies of men, women, and children. The misery was indescribable.

It was then that I first began to understand the brutality of war. Burned into my memory is the sight of a young mother, probably in her twenties, a baby on her back and a three- or four-year-old child clasped tightly in her arms. Caught against a girder of the bridge, her body bobbed idly in the gentle current.

The stench of the dead bodies was already overpowering in the heat of the midsummer sun. It was a living hell. But compared with what I saw as I approached the area around Hiroshima Station, those who had died were fortunate. In a moment houses had been shattered and their inhabitants buried in a welter of tiles and plaster, their naked bodies covered in ashes. Here and there an arm or a leg protruded. Other bodies lay strewn about, their stomachs torn open and their entrails pouring into the ashes. Often I only realized there was a dead body in the ashes when I stepped on it. The expressions on the dead faces as they gazed emptily into space were more contorted and agonized than those of the fierce gate-guardian deities of Japanese temples.

It was utterly impossible to think of these dead people as peacefully at rest. Some of the bodies made me think that even being in hell itself, your tongue being pulled out, your eyes gouged out, and your ears chopped off, was preferable. But it was worse for those who remained alive for several hours, or even two or three days. When I saw people dying in such pain that they no longer even knew who they were, I could only think that those who had died immediately were far better off.

Most people had been wearing light summer shirts that morning. But most of the dead were bare chested, and many were completely naked, perhaps because their clothes had been burned off them. The parts of the body that had been exposed to the flash had suffered great burns, and the skin was turning purple and trailing from the body in strips.

In every case, the eyeballs of the dead were either protruding from their sockets or hanging out completely. Blood had gushed from the mouth, ears, and nose. The tongue had swelled to the size of a golf ball and had pushed its way out of the mouth, gripped tightly by the teeth. The whole anatomy seemed to have been destroyed. Most bodies were bloated, and it was often impossible to tell whether they were male or female. As friends and relatives began to flock to the scene to search for their loved ones, they were rarely able to identify the bodies just by looking at them.

Hundreds of those still alive were wandering around vacantly. Some were half-dead, writhing in their misery. Others were shuffling along like forlorn ghosts, terrible burns covering more than half the body, the skin of face and arms peeling off and flapping around them. Some were roaming around lost, crying out for water; but when someone called out to them, they seemed not to hear, perhaps because their eardrums had burst. They were no more than living corpses.

Wherever a puddle of water had collected from burst water pipes, people had gathered like ants around a honey pot. Many had died where they lay at the water's edge, their strength gone. Others had clambered over the dead bodies to get at the water, only to die in the same way, their bodies piling one on top of another. There was no medicine and no doctors, nothing but the fierce summer heat.

Even today, so many years later, it gives me a chill to think about what happened. On the second day, relief trucks came into the city, distributing white potatoes and sweet potatoes in the area around Hiroshima Station. When the trucks arrived, a great crowd of people gathered instantaneously. People wolfed the food down as soon as they received it, not stopping even to wash the dirt off. I remember thinking then that I had had enough of war.

In all the wide plaza in front of the station only one three-story building was still standing, though not a pane of glass was left in its windows. The station was a hollow space, the roof completely gone, all the platforms burned, and only two or three pillars still standing. The area to the north was completely burned out, and near the point of impact to the south, I was told, everything had melted; nothing at all remained. The mountains to the north, with their mantle of pines, were a deep brown, as if a brush fire had swept through them.

I climbed to the roof of a remaining building. On all sides the only buildings left were those built in the Western style. As I looked around, the extent of the destruction came home to me. The ruin was as bad as the terrible damage caused by the air raids in the Osaka-Kobe area. There was an air-raid warden's post nearby, and I talked to three firefighters. They told me that some of their crew who had been on duty that morning had been blown right across the expanse of railway lines to the north side of the station by the blast. I noticed that pieces of scalp were sticking to the sides of the parapet.

I met some people who had come from Okayama to search for their relatives. "We searched and searched but couldn't find where my brother's house used to be. We decided it must be around here and started digging away the ash and plaster. We discovered the bodies of four people, parents and children, sitting as if gathered around a table. They were completely burned, just skeletons. It was only by the cups and other objects in the house that we remembered that we could identify them.'' The memory of the relatives collecting the bones and putting them into a cloth bag still fills me with pain and pity.

One of my most precious keepsakes is the pair of army-issue shoes I wore that day as I walked through the ashes, stepping on the dead. While giving thanks that I am still alive, I pray for the souls of the tens of thousands who were sacrificed.

Weeds by the Roadside

Katsuyoshi Yoshimura

In August 1945 I was in the first grade of primary school. My house was about 1.8 kilometers from the hypocenter, at the approach to Tsurumi Bridge. This bridge spans the Kyobashi River, a tributary of the Ota River that skirts Hijiyama Park. Along the embankment was a road five or six meters wide, which our house faced. From the road the house looked as though it had only one story, but from below it could be seen to have two floors. Our entrance hall was on the second floor, and we usually entered and left by that, going down a staircase in the center of the house to the rooms below. There was a veranda on the first floor and a skylight, so that we could sit in the half-underground living room and look up at the sky. This was where I was sitting that morning when with my own eyes I saw the B-29 drop the bomb.

I should have gone to school on August 6, 1945. Air raids had disrupted our schooling, so we had given up our summer vacation to attend classes. It may have been luck or the grace of God, but that morning I had a stomachache and was nagging my mother to let me stay home. She was telling me to put up with it and go to school, and promised to take me to the Shukkeien garden afterward as a treat. I had a lot of stomach trouble at that time and missed school quite often, and I think my mother was slightly impatient with me.

My mother was sitting on the edge of the veranda, shelling peas, and I was sitting in the middle of the room with the skylight, having out the question of school with her. One of our neighbors came by with potatoes and onions and seated herself on the veranda to chat with my mother. I was half-listening to their conversation when through the skylight I noticed two planes, small in the clear summer sky. As I watched, fascinated, I saw something white fall from one of them and then was blinded by a brilliant flash. About five seconds passed. Then a great noise exploded, as if to shake the ground itself.

"Katsu, it's a bomb!" cried my mother and flew in from the veranda to where I was sitting. She threw herself on top of me just as the blast hit us. The house collapsed around us, and we were buried under the debris. The ceiling and the furniture from the second floor fell around us. It seemed like a long time but was probably only ten or fifteen minutes before things stopped falling and everything grew quiet. We were enveloped in darkness.

It seems strange to think of it now, but my mother, pulling me with her, unerringly burrowed out into the open. It is a complete mystery to me how she managed to do it, but it was our one piece of good fortune in all the terrors of that day. If we had not been able to get out, we would have been trapped by the fires from the neighboring houses and would have been burned alive. There had been someone else with us at the time of the blast, the woman with the vegetables, but in the ensuing chaos both my mother and I had completely forgotten about her.

As soon as we got outside, we saw my brother, then four years old. He had been sitting by the roadside at the time of the blast, watching the umbrella mender work. He told us later that the blast had thrown the man four or five meters into the air before he crashed to the ground. He had not moved again. Though my brother had been sitting beside the umbrella mender, he had not been blown into the air but had just continued to sit there alone. He was burned on the right side of his head and on his right arm and still bears the keloids, although he is in perfect health.

The three of us waited for my father and sisters to come home, and we rejoiced when we found that we were all safe and sound. Perhaps it was about two hours after the blast that my mother remembered the neighbor and told my father. He immediately went into the ruins of the house to look for her. He finally discovered her trapped under the lintel of the back door, unable to move. Using all his strength, he pulled it off her. If my mother had remembered even a little later, the woman would probably have been burned alive, since the fires were moving faster now. After that the woman always referred to my father as her savior. What has happened to her, where she is now, I do not know.

There were seven of us living in Hiroshima at the time. My older brother, fourteen years my senior, was serving in the army in China, while an older sister had been sent to our aunt's in Kumamoto, on the southern island of Kyushu. Still in Hiroshima were my parents, my grandmother, two older sisters, my younger brother, and I. The only one who had not come back home was my eighty-year-old grandmother. That morning she had taken her year-old great-granddaughter, my cousin's child, to nearby Hijiyama Park to play.

When noon had come and there was still no sign of my grandmother, my father went to the park to look for her. He found her crouching over the dead baby. Since she was exhausted, he put her on his back and sadly returned home. She died two days later.

Whenever I think of what happened next, I can hardly write for emotion. The landscape around me looked like a scene from a medieval painting of hell. There was a woman, her entire body burned and almost completely naked, whose skin was hanging down from her face in strips. A woman was fleeing, still clutching her dead child to her breast. Children were crying for their mothers. A person had toppled over dead while crying for water. I can still see the scene vividly, so deeply was it burned into my seven-year-old eyes.

That evening a soldier came by and distributed rice balls to the people in the neighborhood. Although they were only sprinkled with salt, at the time they were more delicious than the most extravagant banquet fare. My house had already burned down and was now smoldering. Our valuables, which had been placed in a neighbor's storehouse for safekeeping, were also lost, since neither the owner nor the key could be found before the fire took hold and burned our possessions before our eyes. This was a matter of lasting regret to my mother. We had been unable to rescue many of our household effects before our house went up, either. I spent the night sleeplessly, looking vacantly out over the ruins.

The next day my father made a rough shelter for us. He was very clever at that sort of thing. In a day he had a shack built for us, a crude affair not much bigger than nine square meters. When I look back on it, I feel that to have been able to do such a thing in that wasteland was quite extraordinary. The six of us lived there for about two months.

Those two months seemed unending to me. Day in, day out, I would sit by the road selling household goods—cups, plates, and bowls—that father had dug up from the garden where he had buried them for safety. It seems stupid, thinking about it now, to have set up shop in such conditions, but at the time it was the one thing that I could do.

All day I would sit by the road, but many days I would sell nothing or just one thing. But because my father told me to, I would sit there in the blazing heat every day. I have very little recollection of how my parents and sisters found the food that we ate. Nevertheless, the difficult days went by. The people around us kept dying, and every day the cremation fires burned on the other side of the river. Each evening we could hear the bugles blown by the soldiers and smell the indescribable odor of burning flesh.

Even now I remember the stench of the dead bodies decaying as they remained uncollected for days in the scorching heat. The body of an unidentified man was lying near our house. He had been calling for water repeatedly, and after he died he was just left lying where he had fallen, face upward, with bubbles break-

ing from his nose and mouth. Why he was just left there I do not
know.

In October we went to live with my aunt in Kumamoto. Both
my parents died the next year, and after a year in Kumamoto
my older brother took us back to Hiroshima, where we lived in a
house he had built on the ruins of the previous one.

Being orphans, we did not have an easy life. I was eight, and
my younger brother was five. My oldest sister soon married, and
my older brother, too. My other sisters helped with the family
finances by working as housemaids. In this way the six of us
grew up together in poverty on Hiroshima's tainted soil, hardy
weeds in the wasteland.

A Nurse in Hiroshima

Sakae Hosaka

After I finished school, I went to Osaka. Living and working at the small ear, nose, and throat clinic of an acquaintance, I worked for my nursing qualification, which I received two years later. Some time after that the doctor at the clinic was called up and sent to the front. I thought he would soon be back and in the meantime went to live at the clinic of a good friend of his. As it became more and more apparent that the doctor would not be returning for a considerable time, I went to work in a military hospital in Hiroshima Prefecture at the invitation of a former classmate.

The hospital, a specialized institution for tubercular soldiers, was in the town of Ono, near the island of Miyajima, one of Japan's most scenic spots. My family had made me promise to stay there no more than three years. At the end of that time I went to work at a military-run cooperative hospital near Hiji-yama Park in Hiroshima.

This hospital treated both military personnel and civilians. There were isolation wards for contagious diseases, a gynecology department, and outpatient service. Compared with the Ono hospital, it was a complex institution. I lived for a while in the nurses' dormitory there but later rented a house with my dormitory roommate. Even after we both married, she continued living with us, since her husband was a sailor on the battleship *Yamato* and was rarely home.

On the morning of August 6 an air-raid alert sounded just after seven, when I was in the midst of flurried preparations for work. The all-clear soon sounded, however, and I left the house at my usual time. It was when I was squatting down putting on my work shoes in the changing room at the hospital that the brilliant flash came.

I clearly remember seeing the flash through the window, but nothing else remains in my memory. I fainted. When I came to, I found myself buried under the blankets used by nurses on the night shift. The blankets had been piled on top of the lockers, and when the lockers toppled over, the blankets must have tumbled down neatly on top of me.

I was terrified and went out into the corridor. The interior of the hospital was transformed. Tiles, plaster, glass, chips of wood had fallen and made a great mound on one side of the corridor. As I began to regain my sense of who and where I was, I grew aware of the patients' screams for help. However, the doctors were not yet at the hospital, and there seemed nothing to do but wait. Then I thought of taking some of the patients to the air-raid shelter and, after doing so, ran outside.

There the tragedy of the atomic bombing was spread before my eyes. Five or six little boys, seven or eight years old, came running up, their bodies trembling, and begged me for medicine. "It's so hot!" they cried. I saw that the skin on the upper half of their bodies was peeling off and hanging in strips that looked just like the skin you scrape off a new potato. Abruptly I asked them, "Did you go out without shirts?" They were wearing absolutely nothing above the waist. "We were wearing shirts," they replied. When I looked carefully, I could see the remnants of their clothes embedded in their upper bodies. I quickly dressed the burns as best I could.

Looking back toward the hospital, I saw that outpatients had suddenly begun to congregate. Injured people were lying wherever there was room, in the corridors or on the concrete floor of the entrance hall, so that there was hardly room to walk. Most of the injured were suffering burns, but in no time our stock of medicine was exhausted, and all I could do was walk around with a bottle of olive oil, painting the wounds with a brush. We asked the names of the injured, posted them on a noticeboard outside the hospital, and rushed around trying to get water for those who were crying out for it. Very often we were too late, and by the time we came back the person was beyond help. It is impossible to describe the scene. I can only compare it to hell.

There were only about half the usual number of regulars at work that day, and few of the doctors were there. When I think back, we were not really functioning as a hospital. I have no idea how we managed.

Several hours passed. I felt as if I were in a trance. Toward evening my husband came to meet me and we set off for home. I was worried that our house had burned down, but luckily it had escaped the fires. I found it strange that although we were without electric light, the house looked bright inside. When I went in, all I could see was mud—the tatami floor mats had completely disappeared. At first I could not understand what had happened, but when I had recovered my calm and could look around properly, I realized that the blast had blown off the roof. The ceiling had fallen cleanly into one place, and we could see the stars above. The tatami mats were buried centimeters deep under fallen objects. That night we remained on the alert for further air raids, staying outside in the street with our neighbors. None of us slept a wink.

The next day we discharged all patients who could possibly return home. All those remaining were people who had been injured in the bombing. Although technically we had admitted them, there were not enough beds for all, and most patients had to be placed on the floor.

As the days passed, the mass of patients gradually diminished. The hospital, which had been full of sound, grew silent. Everyone was dying. A bonfire was built in a vacant lot near the hospital, and the bodies were piled on it. Oil was poured over them and ignited. Each day more and more of the vast crowd of people became ashes. Only a peculiar smell remained. Such a thing could no longer arouse emotion. Our feelings were numb.

We moved to Konoura on Etajima, an island about ten kilometers south of Hiroshima, where my husband's unit of the Kamikaze Special Attack Force was stationed, and I commuted to the hospital by boat. Before many days had passed, however, I began to run a fever, and since it did not subside, I found myself too weak to continue at the hospital. For some reason I could not discover, a rash appeared on my body, and my eyesight began to fail. When I think about it now, I realize it was probably due to the atomic bomb. At the time somebody had said it would be seventy years before any plants would grow again in Hiroshima.

While I was resting at Konoura, a relative of one of the officers in my husband's unit was brought to us suffering from burns and the effects of radiation. The burns covered more than half his body, and maggots were breeding in them. Though we removed as many maggots as we could, more remained, a moving mass beneath his pale skin. He suffered greatly, but there was no effective treatment we could give him. The most pitiful thing about it, when I think back, was our powerlessness to do anything.

The terrible thing about radiation is that nobody knows how or when it will make its effects felt. I have known someone who had virtually no health problems in thirty years die suddenly of leukemia. Whenever I fall ill, I am afraid I will never get well again. My husband, also a victim of the bombing, contracted pulmonary tuberculosis in 1947, and it cost him the most important time of his life. He is now suffering from diabetes and is resigned to having illness as his companion the rest of his days.

Our life since moving to Tokyo in 1949 has not been easy. Our daughter, born in 1948, has been anemic since childhood. Many times she has almost fainted when taking a bath and has had to have injections. The problem became more severe when she reached adulthood. When she married and became pregnant, she was advised by the doctor to take a dietary supplement, since there might be complications at the baby's birth.

I have suffered from pains in the lower half of my body for more than twenty years, and when I stand up suddenly, things go black. I am fearful when I hear people talk of preparing for old age. Right now we can do little but try to make the present a little brighter for ourselves.

Is it right that people should make weapons that could destroy all life on this planet? We are now over sixty. We will continue to warn of the dangers while we can still move, but we need the help of the young. Take over where we leave off!

The Unforgivable

Teiichi Teramura

The atomic bomb that appeared in the clear summer sky on August 6, 1945, destroyed the city of Hiroshima in an instant. The damage in bare figures was 13.2 square kilometers destroyed by fire, 200,000 people killed or missing (out of a population of 310,000), 31,000 people injured, 57,000 homes totally destroyed, and 15,000 homes partially destroyed.

When I rushed to Hiroshima that day as part of the rescue operation, I experienced directly the tragedy, atrocity, and inhumanity of the bomb. The experience was so appalling that it destroyed utterly the numbness to misery I had developed on numerous battlefields.

That spring I had been evacuated by submarine from the terrible front in eastern New Guinea to staff one of the skeleton units that were being formed to defend the Japanese islands in the expected Allied invasion. I was appointed a field officer with the 52d Ship Construction Battalion based at Murotsu in Yamaguchi Prefecture, about forty-five miles from Hiroshima.

I was at the battalion headquarters in the early afternoon of August 6 when a telegram arrived from our commander informing us that a bomb of an unknown type had fallen on Hiroshima that morning and caused great destruction. I was ordered to the

stricken city to provide emergency relief. Tormented by an
ominous foreboding, I set out by a fast boat. Night had fallen by
the time I reached the port of Ujina in Hiroshima.

I alighted at the pier, since I was under orders to report to our
headquarters there. As I stepped onto the jetty, however, I in-
voluntarily came to a halt. I could see nothing clearly in the
darkness, but the air around me reeked of blood and death.
Then moaning assaulted my ears and made them ring as if a vast
number of scales were being played together. I realized to my
horror that all around me were thousands of wounded people, lying on the cold concrete waiting for death. They had been placed
there because there was nowhere for them to go, and none of
them were receiving any medical attention. They were living
corpses in a hell on earth, with only the peace of death to hope
for. Though I wanted to do something for them, I realized
bitterly that nothing could help them now.

The next morning the headquarters was shifted to the ruins of
the mansion of Marquis Asano, near the hypocenter, and we
moved upstream by boat. Most of the houses in Ujina had
escaped total destruction, but virtually all were deserted. And
Hiroshima itself . . . I could not believe what I saw. Was this the
beautiful city that had preserved hundreds of years of tradition?
In the streets not a tree or a blade of grass remained. Only a
blackened desolation spread out before me.

Some modern buildings retained their shape, but their concrete walls had crumbled, and the steel girders, laid bare, were
leaning away from the hypocenter. The roads were strewn with
the fire-blackened corpses of people, horses, and dogs. Survivors
were walking around stupefied.

Corpses filled not only the streets but also the many rivers and
the nameless canals and creeks. Several hundred bodies had
even floated as far as Hiroshima Bay. It was our battalion's job
to recover those bodies from the water.

We had to pull the charred bodies aboard with ropes and then
take them ashore, where others were waiting to deal with them.
There was no way of distinguishing the bodies by sex or age.
Most had completely lost their clothes, and all were brown and

swollen. Their skin had peeled off and hung dangling, like the peelings of a bruised, black loquat, and all their hair had fallen out. We would load five or six bodies aboard and then head back. In this weird landscape, the soldiers preserved a deep silence in the face of the brutality around them.

Ashore, the bodies were piled into heaps and set alight. Smoke rose from all points of the devastated land, like bridges carrying the souls of the dead to heaven. At night the flames from the pyres could be seen all about, making me think that the spirits had become will-o'-the-wisps.

The family of a lieutenant general with the army supply depot in Ujina had been living in the Asano mansion, where we were bivouacked. The beautiful garden had been completely burned; only the centuries-old pines remained, blown down and stripped of their leaves. This showed just how strong the blast had been.

The general had been on his way to work when the bomb fell. He had escaped with only light injuries, but his family had been trapped under the collapsed house. His wife was calling out to her two daughters, and the girls to their mother, when the cruel flames approached. There was nothing they could do. Unable to free themselves, they were burned alive.

"She looked after the girls so well. I pray that she will take them by the hand and lead them across the river of death. Hail Amida Buddha!" The next day the general, his face streaming with tears, gathered together the charred bones that were all that remained of his beloved wife and children. However exalted a person he was, however much a soldier, in the end he was an ordinary human being, a husband and father. We could say nothing, only stand with bowed heads.

On August 8, 1945, the Soviet Union declared war on Japan. The next day, Nagasaki was bombed.

The situation became ever more critical. It was announced that the Allied forces were about to land on the Japanese mainland. Our detachment was relieved from rescue operations in Hiroshima and sent back to our original base to continue the work we had been doing. We arrived back in Murotsu on August 10. This important, thriving port on the Inland Sea commanded a strategic position in terms of water traffic. Murotsu Bay was an excellent natural harbor, and eminently suitable as a fleet anchorage. Our detachment was posted in this strategic spot. Our orders were to build transportation facilities and a place of concealment for ships.

August 12 was a day of intense heat. The land sweltered under a sultry sun, and it seemed as if everything would evaporate. About two o'clock a woman's cry, a sound like silk rending, suddenly reverberated above the piercing noise of the cicadas. I went outside to see what was the matter. There I found two women weeping in each other's arms.

I saw two or three people from the neighborhood run up to them and, realizing that something out of the ordinary had happened, hurried over. One of the women was a widow who lived locally. Her son was in the army in the Pacific, and her daughter had married and gone to live in Hiroshima. I had heard that her daughter, who was spoken of highly as an excellent wife, was her pride and joy. When the bomb fell, it was as if the light had gone out of her life.

No news of the daughter came, and every day the mother prayed to the gods and buddhas for her safety. She had come asking us for information when we returned from Hiroshima, but all we could do was try to reassure her with conventional phrases that her daughter had surely fled to safety somewhere. This did not comfort her.

What I now saw was the homecoming of Sachiko, the daughter. Although she had arrived home safely, she was a pathetic sight. Her clothes were in rags, her long black hair had been burned so that now she was almost bald, her eyes were puffed up, and her face was burned. She was a sight pitiful beyond words.

Despite her injuries, she had found her way back to her mother's house. It was like a miracle. Going as often as not without food, intent only on reaching her mother, she had joined a group of victims leaving the city. Kind people had helped her along the way. What will it must have taken for her to arrive safely in her mother's arms!

What had happened to that smiling young wife? The mother looked at her child, now more an apparition than a woman, and wept, cursing the war and the atomic bomb.

"Mother, don't cry so. I am a soldier's wife, and I can face him now. I am ashamed, though, because his parents died and I am still alive," she said, comforting her mother. I felt as if I were watching a living Buddha, so noble and exalted did she look.

I took her immediately to the army doctor for treatment. That was the greatest kindness I did at that time. Even the army was in short supply of medical goods. To the mother and daughter, it must have been like receiving help in hell. They brought the palms of their hands together in thanks. Sachiko was given an all-important injection of Ringer's solution, as well as ointment for her burns, and as treatment continued, she began to regain her grip on life.

The years flowed by. In September 1955 I took a trip to Yamaguchi Prefecture and visited Murotsu again. The abandoned ships that had been left lying in the bay at the war's end had been towed away and disposed of. The port had returned to prosperity as a fishing and transport center and was bustling with activity. The children who had helped entertain the battalion at the primary school were now adults, taking their places in society. It was truly a happy ending.

The light in the lighthouse on the cape was still burning as it always had, but otherwise the past seemed to have been obliterated. However, the tunnels that we had labored night and day to build to hide ships could still be seen, half-collapsed and overgrown, telling mutely of the past.

On the surface, the cruel wounds of war had disappeared, but in actual fact they could never be erased from the little fishing town, now in its tenth year of peace. Sachiko, the young woman who had escaped from the atomic bombing, had committed suicide by walking into the sea.

An old woman in the town told me, "Both the son and

Sachiko's husband died in the war, and the mother and daughter lived together alone. They must have found it hard going in the difficult times that followed the war. . . . Anyway, somehow or other Sachiko got well, and although she suffered because of the loss of her husband and brother, five years or so passed calmly enough. But both mother and daughter suffered because the keloids wouldn't go away. In fact they seemed to grow deeper and more pronounced as the years passed.'' (This was not a problem these two alone faced; all the victims of the atomic bombing experienced the same thing.) The old woman continued, ''And what was even more pitiful was that incurable radiation sickness began to spread through Sachiko's body. Finally she lost her will to live and just walked into the sea.''

Deeply moved, I prayed for Sachiko's happiness in the next world and then left the town. The wild chrysanthemums in the fields outside Murotsu were quivering in the wind, the blue sea of the bay sparkling behind them.

When I think back, I realize that from the time of the China Incident in 1937, when I was conscripted at the age of twenty-one, until the end of the war in 1945, I was always at the command of my draft card, never off duty. I fought as a junior officer in China, on the fierce battlefields of the southern front, and in what were probably the grimmest battles of the war, in Guadalcanal and eastern New Guinea. Somehow or other I survived. It was with the experience of the Hiroshima bombing that I ended the decade of my twenties.

It must never happen again!

A Child's Hiroshima

Kiyoko Sato

Until I was in the third grade of primary school I lived in Tokyo, but in March 1945 the family moved to the Ujina district of Hiroshima because of my father's work. Shortly after that, all primary school children in the third grade and up were evacuated. Parting from my parents and my seven brothers and sisters, I went with my teachers and classmates to a temple in the countryside at Miyoshi. For food we had only potatoes and gruel made with rice and vegetables, and I felt hungry all the time.

On the morning of August 6, when I was cleaning the main hall of the temple, I felt a vibration, and happening to look up in the direction of the mountains behind which Hiroshima lay, I saw plumes of dense black smoke rising. It reminded me of a brush fire. The next day one of the older pupils, who had gone to help out on a nearby farm, heard that a massive bomb had been dropped on Hiroshima. I was anxious about my family, but my teachers said nothing about the bomb.

About six days later the man who lived next door to our house in Hiroshima arrived to see me, having walked all night. He told me that my mother was very sick and that I should return with him. Early the next morning, carrying two potatoes for lunch and with two pairs of straw sandals I had made myself strapped to my back, I set out to return home with our neighbor as my guide. It was about one hundred kilometers to Hiroshima from the temple, and since there were no trains running, we had to walk the whole way. I plodded on, in a daze of happiness over returning home.

We arrived in Hiroshima after night had fallen. I will never forget what I saw in the streets of the city. There was no sound or light anywhere, and no life disturbed the dead streets. What was more frightening than anything else was the sight, in the moonlight, of the skeleton of a burned-out streetcar with its load of fire-blackened passengers. One corpse was still clinging to a strap. I could see trails of silvery phosphorus weaving all about, for all the world like the spirits of the dead in my storybooks. I closed my eyes to shut out the horror and, clinging to our neighbor's hand, went on to Ujina and home.

Only three members of the family were there when I arrived. My oldest brother was lying down, unable to move, his entire body pierced with slivers of glass. The tip of a younger brother's nose had been torn off, and a bandage covered his face. They told me that my mother had been taken to the aid station at Itsukaichi and that my father and older sister were there with her. My mother had been serving in the women's volunteer labor corps, doing demolition work in front of the city office, when the bomb fell.

The next morning I set off again with an older brother. Arriving at the aid station, I searched the rooms one by one for my mother. In one room I saw dozens of people on the floor, moaning in pain. Eventually I found my father and sister and ran to them. My sister was covering my mother's face with a square of white linen, and my father told me she had just died. If I had only walked a little faster, I would have been in time! I was distressed that I had not been able to see her alive and cried loudly. My mother's face was covered in blisters and had swollen to twice its normal size, and her hair had fallen out. She was unrecognizable as the mother I had known so well.

One of my older brothers, who had been at morning parade at his school when the bomb fell, had suffered burns over his entire body and had died shortly before my mother.

We cremated my mother and returned to our home in Ujina. In front of our house, the dead bodies of people who had been fleeing from the hypocenter were lying where they had fallen. Since it was midsummer, the smell was horrible. My brother put the bodies into drawers from our clothes chests before taking them away for cremation.

My oldest brother died in October. After that my father began to act more and more strangely, and one day he went out somewhere and never came home again. His place was taken by another brother who had just been demobilized as disabled. He pushed his undernourished body to the limit, often working as a black marketeer to support us. The following January he died from overwork. My family now consisted of an older sister just turned twenty-one, a younger brother, and me.

It was a time of severe food shortages, when survival was difficult even for adults. We children subsisted by raiding deserted military food stores and selling the stolen items on the black market. I was supposed to be at primary school, but instead of going to school I tried to help my sister by steaming potatoes and selling them in front of Hiroshima Station. Somehow the three of us survived.

The ten years after the end of the war were the real war for me. As an orphan, I received no help from the government. Because my main concern was staying alive, I received hardly any education. But I survived.

This year I am the same age that my mother was when she died. I have a son and a daughter at university and a child in middle school. At last I think I understand how my mother must have felt, knowing that death was going to take her from us. I hope my children will never have to experience the sorrow I did.

Hiroshima, early October 1945. This photograph, looking south, was taken from a point about two hundred meters from the hypocenter (at the left near the junction of two streets). The Industrial Promotion Hall (now the Atomic Bomb Dome) can be seen on the right. (Photo by Shigeo Hayashi)

Nagasaki, August 10, 1945. This photograph was taken near the hypocenter. Charred corpses strew the foreground area. (Photo by Yosuke Yamahata)

Hiroshima, August 6 These are among the only five known photographs—all taken by the same person—recording conditions in Hiroshima on the day of the bombing. *Opposite: Near Miyukibashi bridge, about 2.2 kilometers from the hypocenter, at around 11:00 A.M. In the background is a police substation. Below, a policeman applies cooking oil to burns. Above: About 2.7 kilometers from the hypocenter, sometime in the afternoon. A policeman, his head bandaged, issues certificates entitling people to emergency rations. (Photos by Yoshito Matsushige)*

Nagasaki, August 9. This is the only known photograph taken the day of the bombing. People are fleeing the vicinity of Nagasaki Station. (Photo courtesy of the Hiroshima-Nagasaki Publishing Committee)

Nagasaki, August 10. Below: Relief workers and other people searching for survivors pick their way through the rubble about seven hundred meters from the hypocenter. Opposite: Dazed and dying victims sit or lie on the ground about 1.5 kilometers from the hypocenter. (Photos by Yosuke Yamahata)

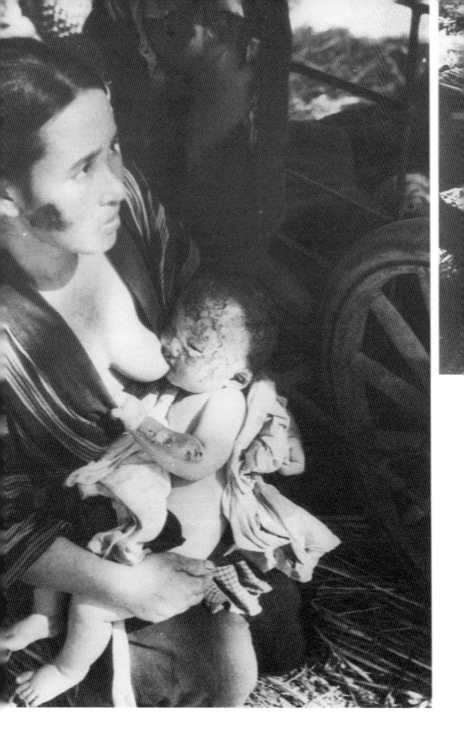

Nagasaki, August 10. The area in front of Michinoo Station, about 3.5 kilometers from the hypocenter, has become an emergency aid station. Opposite: A woman feeds her baby as she waits her turn for treatment by doctors and nurses from the Omura navy hospital. Above: Two babies receive first aid for burns. (Photos by Yosuke Yamahata)

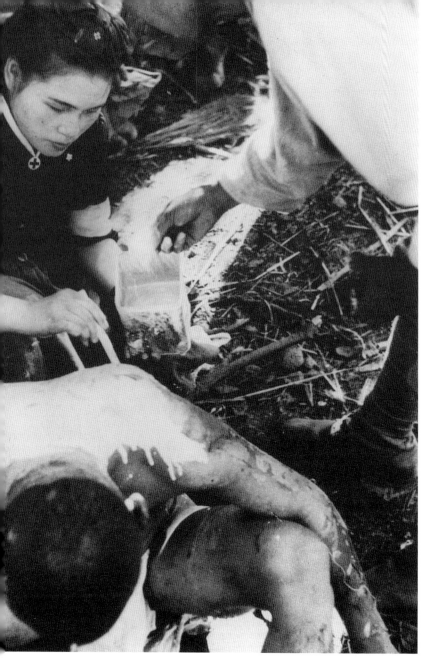

Nagasaki, August 10. A navy nurse gives first aid for burns. The most seriously injured victims were taken by train to navy hospitals in Omura and Isahaya. (Photo by Yosuke Yamahata)

Hiroshima, August 12. A relief worker tries to give a little girl a cup of water. She is about to be taken by truck to a treatment facility. (Photo by Hajime Miyatake; courtesy of Asahi Shimbun Co.)

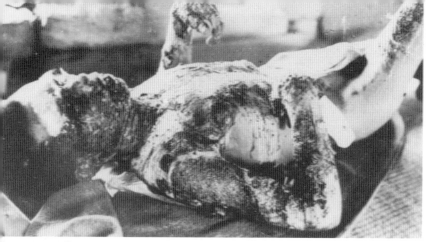

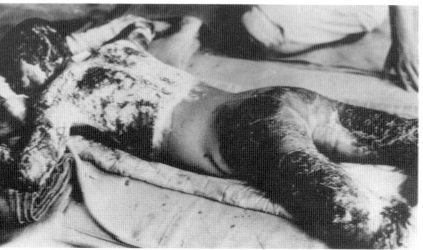

Hiroshima, August 7. Burn victims wait for death to free them from their suffering. (Photos by Masami Onuka)

Opposite: Hiroshima, August 8. The Dai Ichi Primary School, still standing about 2.6 kilometers from the hypocenter, has been made into an improvised hospital. (Photo by Army Marine Division Headquarters)

Hiroshima, August 10. Burns have obliterated the features of this young woman, a student-worker. She died not long after this photo was taken at the Red Cross Hospital. (Photo by Hajime Miyatake; courtesy of Asahi Shimbun Co.)

Opposite: Nagasaki, August 10 or 11. A fourteen-year-old girl, her skin hanging in strips, is brought to the Ōmura navy hospital. (Photo by Masao Shiotsuki, M.D.; courtesy of the Hiroshima-Nagasaki Publishing Committee)

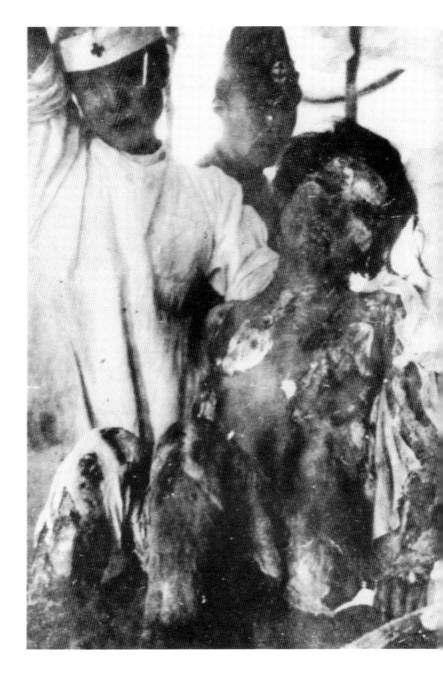

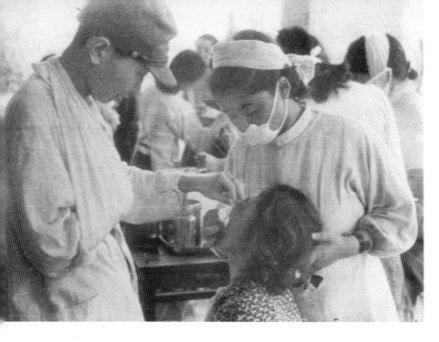

Hiroshima, August 10. Burn victims are treated at the Red Cross Hospital. (Photos by Hajime Miyatake; courtesy of Asahi Shimbun Co.)

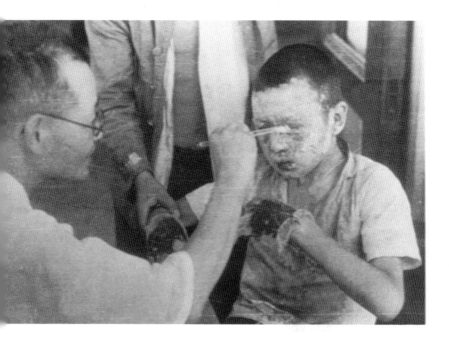

Above: Hiroshima, August 12. Bodies are brought to this site about eight hundred meters from the hypocenter for cremation. (Photo by Hajime Miyatake; courtesy of Asahi Shimbun Co.) Below: Nagasaki, September. About 1.3 kilometers from the hypocenter, a family cremates one of its members. (Photo by Eiichi Matsumoto)

Nagasaki, August 10. A boy carries his injured younger brother on his back as they search for their father near Nagasaki Station. (Photo by Yosuke Yamahata)

A Memorial for the Slaughtered

Akira Nagasaka

When the bomb fell on Nagasaki, I was living with my mother and nine-year-old nephew at Oka-machi in the Urakami district, near Urakami Cathedral and about two hundred meters from the hypocenter. Sixteen at the time and an avid patriot, I had been mobilized as a student-worker.

There had been an air-raid warning on the morning of August 9, and all movement had been temporarily stopped. My mother urged me to stay home that day, but, brushing off her suggestion, I set off for the Kami Nagasaki Primary School, where my work unit was based. The school, located on the east side of a range of low hills that divided Nagasaki into two, was being used by Mitsubishi Steel Works as a branch factory.

At two minutes past eleven there was a blinding flash from all sides, and the glass blew out of all the windows. Everyone fled to the air-raid trenches for shelter, but after about ten minutes we ventured out and looked up at the sky. Over the hills a great ash-colored cloud was rising into the sky as if in slow motion. Our boss surmised that the main factory had been hit, and several dozen workers made their way over the hills to see. The sight that confronted us when we reached the top pulled us up short. Below us was a sea of flame. We could hear the sounds of explosions and the whoosh of the fiery winds that were blowing upward. We were told we could leave, and I set off alone along the ridge that led to my home.

All the trees on the hillside had been uprooted and were lying flat on the ground facing in the same direction. I picked my way through the fallen trees in a daze, compelled by the thought that I had to find my mother. I was about a hundred meters beyond the Nagasaki Medical College Hospital when I suddenly heard a voice at my feet crying out for water. Surprised, I swung around and saw a sight that made me stand transfixed. A woman, probably in her mid-thirties, was lying on the ground, her hair wild, her clothes in tatters, her face red with blood. She was putting all the strength that remained in her to raise her head and murmur, ''Water, water.''

When I had gathered my wits about me, I scooped some dirty water out of a nearby ditch and gave it to her. She drank it as if it were the most delicious thing ever to pass her lips, but most of it merely trickled down her chin onto her breast. ''More, please,'' she begged, but she could do no more than gasp for breath when I brought it, having no strength left to drink.

A few moments passed in silence. Then she looked up at me and asked me to take her home. I did not know what to do. I desperately wanted to find my mother, to discover what had happened to her and my nephew. I did not see how I could cope with an unknown woman on my back. I spun around and ran away. As I fled, I told myself that there was nothing else I could do.

The area around Urakami Cathedral was completely burned out, and the heat prevented me from approaching. It was not until early the next morning that I made my way to what appeared to be the ruins of our house. The whole area was a fire-blackened desolation. There was not even a charred remnant of the huge camphor tree that had stood behind our house. All around me were strewn skeletons, scattered bones, and torsos of ebony ash. I sank down, exhausted. When I had recovered somewhat, I began looking for my mother, or rather, her bones. All I had to go by was the fact that she had had gold teeth. I held skull after skull in my hands and peered into the jaw area. I wonder how many people's skulls I picked up during my search. I continued searching frantically. There were times when, squatting, I even raised fire-blackened heads to look at the teeth. I spent that whole day, the tenth, picking up skulls and putting them down again.

My search continued in the same way for two or three more days. After that, I saw more and more people searching the ruins like me, and relief teams arrived to clear away the bodies. As I was making the rounds of the aid stations in the faint hope that my mother had been accommodated in one, I noticed a newspaper posted on a bulletin board near the Katsuyama Primary School. I read that Nagasaki had been hit by a new type of bomb and had suffered "a little damage." I was shocked. A *little* damage? My blood rose in anger. All around me as far as the eye could see were ruins, and all who had been living were now dead. My mother and my nephew were nowhere to be found. And this was "a little damage"? What kinds of lies were the newspapers reporting?

Until then I had never doubted the veracity of the authorities. I was desperate to be allowed to die for the Emperor. Now I realized that the military and the cabinet, those who had the trust of the Emperor, were openly propagating lies. I yelled, "Liars!" and kicked the bulletin board with all my strength. It was a futile gesture and did nothing to relieve the emptiness that overwhelmed me.

That day and the next I continued searching for my mother's bones, taking up skull after skull, but in vain. Meanwhile, the clearing away of bodies continued. I wandered around, often crying aloud as I walked.

My father had died when I was six, and my mother had reared my brothers and me single-handedly. Maybe because I was the youngest child, she lavished extra affection on me. In March 1944, after my brothers had all gone off to war, I came down with meningitis, which left me with a bad leg. Her love and concern for me grew even greater. On August 9, when we had all been warned to stay indoors, she had wanted me to remain at home for the day out of concern for my health. And now I could not even find her teeth. She had died that day, worrying about me; and I, who had shrugged off her concern, remained alive. My mother and nephew had been killed just because they happened to be in Urakami. Their bodies had probably vaporized in the seven-thousand-degree heat.

After the war I was taken in by the family of a close friend who lived in the Mogi-machi district. There I found work as a substitute teacher. I was drawn to study, however, and in 1948 I took myself off to Tokyo. My scholarship money was not enough to cover my school fees and living expenses, and I worked day in, day out doing manual labor. I even sold my blood to help make ends meet.

Eventually I found work as a teacher in Itabashi Ward, Tokyo, in 1951, but my life had no real stability. Nevertheless, I married and had children. One day I happened to learn that the Stockholm Appeal of 1950 had played a major role in the antinuclear movement. I began to feel that I had a duty to discharge, for the sake of my children, as a living witness to the cruelty of the atomic bomb.

What pained me most was the memory of the unknown woman I had abandoned. I reproached myself for not having taken her with me, and however much I tried to reason with myself that she would have died anyway from the radiation, I continued to suffer from guilt. There are times even now when an unguarded look at my hands brings memories rushing back into my mind of that day in hell when I took up skull after skull in the search for my mother's gold teeth, and when I abandoned the woman with the blood-covered face.

Gradually, however, I began to feel that I could make a true memorial to that unknown woman by speaking of the pain and suffering that she had gone through. I began to campaign for a ban on nuclear weapons. The conviction that atomic weapons were unforgivable grew ever stronger as I watched children of atomic bomb survivors die, first a six-year-old girl in my neighborhood from a brain tumor, then a favorite student, seventeen years old, from cancer of the liver.

The situation in Japan today is dubious. Articles and photographs concerning peace have been withdrawn from publicly funded textbooks, and literary materials designed to deepen the awareness of these things have been unjustifiably attacked. F-16 jet fighters capable of carrying nuclear missiles have been based at Misawa at America's request, and Japan is steadily rearming. I find little difference between this and the government's attitude in 1945 when it deceived the people of Japan about "a little damage" to Nagasaki on that day of fire and desolation and urged that we continue fighting. I wonder how the government, whose duty it is to protect citizens' lives and property, regards the damage that nuclear weapons can cause?

I will continue to cry out against all nuclear weapons while I have any life in me, for the sake of the mother and nephew whose bones I never found and for the sake of that woman who died alone.

A Relief Worker in Hiroshima

Nakaichi Nakamura

I was with one of the first relief teams to enter Hiroshima on August 6, 1945. The thriving city of just twenty-four hours earlier had been reduced to rubble on which countless dead bodies lay strewn about or piled on top of one another. Here and there we could hear voices crying out plaintively for help. Fires were raging, and the earth was as hot as if it had been baked. A scene terrible beyond description spread before my eyes. It was hell recreated on earth.

Our work began with aid to the injured. As dawn approached, appeals for protection against the cold arose from all sides. We covered people with all the blankets we had, but even so, when morning came at last, we discovered that half were already dead.

All the containers of water for fire fighting were crammed with the bodies of those who had sought water in which to escape the encroaching fires. There were many young women, possibly members of the women's work units. It was impossible to pull out the burned and swollen bodies. Finally we had to break the walls of the containers with mallets. As we did so, the bodies tumbled out.

Smeared with blood and dirt, we picked up the bodies that lay wherever we looked, hoisted them on our backs, and loaded them onto whatever boards we could find that had escaped the fires. The collection of corpses continued until late at night. When we found a suitable vacant lot, we dug a huge hole and lined the bottom with pieces of wood. Onto these we gently lowered about fifty bodies—swollen, stomachs gaping open, eyeballs gone, many the torn bodies of young children—and set fire to them. We stood around them as they burned and did not move until the flames had died away.

We rescued people still trapped under fallen buildings, shouldered corpses out of the river, and treated the maggot-infested wounds of the injured. This work continued for about a week. When people are in extreme circumstances, they seem to lose all feeling. Their minds and bodies grow numb, preventing them from thinking about what they are experiencing. All capacity for tears and grief had vanished from my being.

Night approached at last. I saw someone shuffling along, bathed in the evening sun. As the figure approached, I made out a young woman of twenty-four or twenty-five, her body covered with festering burns, her skin dangling in strips. She was clutching a dead baby to her breast.

"Cure my child," she begged me. I suggested that I treat her first, since her wounds were very serious, but she continued to plead brokenly for me to do something for the child. I told her I would do as she wanted, and took the dead baby in my arms. The moment she was relieved of her burden, the young woman collapsed at my feet. She was already dead when I bent down to her. To save the life of her child she had wandered through fires and over rubble, spurred by the need to seek help. When she had found that help for her child, her need to continue living was gone.

At the end of March 1945 I had been sent to the Konoura base on the island of Etajima, about ten kilometers from Hiroshima, to receive training in the Kamikaze Special Attack Force. I was awaiting my fate, set for August 18, when I would ram a high-speed plywood boat loaded with a 250-kilogram bomb into an enemy ship. I had absolutely no fear of death as a human torpedo. I was nineteen, and convinced that my death would aid my country. But what I saw in Hiroshima was the cruelty of a war that did not hesitate to kill innocent women and children. Looking at the collapsed woman at my feet, I felt the evil of war. For the first time, tears started in my parched eyes.

I was in Hiroshima a week. I snatched sleep on radioactive rubble and wolfed down handfuls of rice grasped in fingers that had clasped the bodies of victims. Luckily, I escaped radiation contamination as well as the death of a human torpedo, and also survived the turmoil of the postwar period.

Today there are enough nuclear weapons to kill humankind several times over. It is crucial that all know the reality of the destruction that these weapons can cause so that the tragedy of Hiroshima and Nagasaki may never be repeated. Raise your voices louder and louder in the demand that nuclear weapons be banned. By doing so you will create a strong force for the peace of the world.

In Memory of My Children

Misue Sagami

This year I will be eighty-three, a lonely survivor of the atomic bombing of Hiroshima. I am living in a special nursing home for the aged in Setagaya Ward, Tokyo. Until now I have never spoken to anyone about my past, not even to the man I married after the war or to his daughters. Though I have neither the experience nor the confidence to relate it adequately, I would like to tell you what I recall.

I was born in 1901 in northern Hiroshima Prefecture. After graduating from school in Hiroshima, I married Katashi Sato in 1922 and settled in a suburb of that city, Higashi Hakushima. We were blessed with two children, Nobuko and Masahiro, but my husband, after fighting tuberculosis for six years, died in 1936 at the age of thirty-five, when Nobuko was eleven and Masahiro five. My mother-in-law, who had been very close to her grandchildren, collapsed from the shock of her son's death, and a year later she too died. Thus there were just the three of us left. I sent Masahiro to live with my mother and rented a house in the Hatchobori district. There I began my new life, fighting alone against heavy odds. I went back to school to learn dressmaking and after finishing the course contracted myself to a dry goods store, where I worked very hard.

When the time came for Masahiro to start primary school, I brought him back to live with us. When Nobuko finished school a little later, she was mobilized and went to work with the Japan Electric Generation and Transmission Company (now the Chugoku Electric Power Company). Masahiro eventually went on to middle school.

Both children showed superior promise, although as their mother I should not say it. Nobuko was highly thought of for her beautiful calligraphy, and when he was three Masahiro was written about in the newspaper as a prodigy who could already read. My own life had been fraught with difficulties, and I put all my hope in my children.

That dream was to be obliterated in a second.

On August 6 we were living with the family of my mother's deceased younger brother in Midori-machi. My uncle's widow was four years younger than I, and there were five children, a son and four daughters. At that time the son was in training at Matsuyama, and the youngest daughter was living with her grandparents in Shimane Prefecture. The oldest daughter was in the army, and the other two were going to school in Hiroshima. That morning at about half past seven Nobuko, Masahiro, and their cousins went off to work and school happily, lunch in hand. At that time Masahiro was in the second year of middle school, and he and his classmates were laboring as student-workers in the city, helping with demolition work.

Nobuko was wearing baggy work trousers and a flower-print blouse, and Masahiro, a shirt and trousers, puttees, and soft work boots called *jikatabi*. They were both carrying padded hoods to protect the head in air raids. I can see them as if it were yesterday, for they never grew any older.

That morning the all-clear had sounded as the children were leaving the house, and everything was eerily still. Overcome by a feeling of strangeness, I was standing in our entrance hall, which faced the road to the south, when suddenly a flash of light darted out and I fled back into the room behind the hall in panic. The wall between the hall and the room collapsed, and with it fell the large chest standing against it. One of the girls, who had been in the room, and I were buried beneath the broken wood. Luckily, we were both able to crawl out, but I found that I had broken my thigh and could not walk. Then my uncle's widow returned from a neighbor's house, covered in blood. She had been standing in the front hall when the glass door blew in and pierced her back with countless slivers of glass.

We were fortunate that nearby was a military hospital, where we knew one of the doctors. He came to treat us at our home. We were living about three kilometers from the hypocenter and our house was neither blown down nor burned. The windows and doors were demolished, however; glass was strewn everywhere and even embedded in the pillars. The tremendous force of the explosion was terrifying.

I could only sit looking vacantly out the paneless window, the glass now powder on the floor. Because we were near a hospital, the road that I looked out on had suddenly become a scene from hell. People covered with blood, naked, their skin hanging from them, were running or walking in the direction of the hospital. It was more than I could bear. Across the street from us had stood a school boardinghouse. I will never forget the sight of people pulling the corpse of an old woman out from under the collapsed brick wall.

By evening none of the children who had set out that morning had come home. Racked with anxiety, I spent a sleepless night in the air-raid shelter opposite our house, and by morning I could not move a muscle. Helpless, I continued to wait. Finally at about eleven in the morning the oldest daughter of the house came back, her entire body blackened. She told us she had walked through the night from the Shukkeien garden. She wept because she could do nothing to help her stricken friends.

There was a rumor that all the first-year and second-year middle school students who had been working in the center of the city, including Masahiro, had been burned to death. Another brother of my mother's who lived nearby went out to search for the children once the fires had died down, but there had been such destruction that the whole area was a featureless wilderness, and there was no way of locating them. The three who had not come home would all have been in this general area, and I knew that it was hopeless. Nevertheless, though I realized I might never find any evidence of what had become of them, I continued to hope for some sign that they were still alive. On August 9 my brother came into the city and went around the aid stations to search among the injured there, but in vain. Finally, with nothing more to be done, he made me a pair of crutches from pieces of wood that were lying around and then took me to where my mother and cousins were living.

There was no transportation to be had, and even now I have no idea how we made our way to Hiroshima Station. Around the station were masses of sufferers lying on the roads, whether dead or alive I had no idea. I shrank in both body and mind from the sight of people lying in a sea of blood, their eyeballs hanging out, flies infesting their wounds and breeding maggots. Even now I cannot bear to see films or exhibitions on the bombing. I can remember its horrors only too well.

We finally boarded a train and rode as far as Yoshida. There was no further transport to be had there, so we set out to walk the remaining three kilometers. As night was closing in, we were met on the road by my mother, who despite her sixty-odd years was dragging a cart behind her. I will never forget the happiness and love I felt for my mother when I found myself riding in that cart. When I think back on it now, it seems strange that my mother should have known when to set out to meet us. There had been no communication from my brother or anyone else.

I began living with my mother, my brother, and his wife. After the surrender on August 15, my aunt from Hiroshima and her family joined our household, making us eight in all. Even in the country, food was short, and life was hard for people who were not farmers. My mother and I sewed pretty bags for the rice that the farmers donated to the Buddhist temple and made thongs for wooden clogs, exchanging our labor for rice. We were able to grow our own potatoes and vegetables.

The pieces of glass that had been embedded in my aunt's back were extracted by the local doctor, a relative, and I was also given injections and other treatment. When my aunt and her family finally went back to her parents' home in Shimane, the house suddenly seemed quiet and lonely. I passed my days mourning the fact that of my own family I alone had been left alive. It was my mother's love that supported me then, and it was only the feeling that I could not let her down by dying before she did that kept me going. Eventually, at my mother's urging, I married a distant relative who had been left a widower and had brought up his two daughters alone. After our marriage in 1948 we went to live in Tokyo.

Life in Tokyo was very difficult, the food shortage still being acute. Despite this, my husband's daughters married, and I began attending a tea-ceremony school a former classmate of mine from Hiroshima had started in the Sangenjaya district. My husband and I also went regularly to haiku study meetings. In 1967, just as I was beginning to feel that my life had finally settled, my husband was stricken with cancer of the lymph and died after a short hospitalization. After that I too began to grow weaker and suffered a heart attack. Now I have to wear a pacemaker.

I have entrusted my body to the superintendent of the hospital and my spirit to the Buddha, and I pray for the peace of the world. I am trying to be cheerful and to avoid growing senile.

I was born in the same month as the atomic bombing of Hiroshima, and each year the nursing home gives me a party to celebrate my birthday. The flowers that I receive I dedicate to the memory of my two children. I think back then on the scenes I saw around Hiroshima Station, and can only pray for peace.

Misue Sagami died of a heart attack in October 1984. She was eighty-three years old.

Pursued by Cries

Asae Miyakoshi

I was twenty-five when the atomic bomb was dropped on Hiroshima. In all the years since then, I have not been able to forget what happened, and it is still very hard for me to talk about it.

At that time both my parents were dead, and my husband had gone off to war. Burned out of our home in Osaka by air raids, my five children, aged between one and four, and I sought refuge with my grandfather in Hiroshima. I had lost the hearing in my left ear as a result of the Osaka bombings.

In Hiroshima I lived at Hiratsuka-cho, 1.8 kilometers from the hypocenter, in a household of ten, including my sixty-nine-year-old grandfather, my sisters, aged twenty-one and eighteen, a sixteen-year-old cousin, and my children.

On the morning of August 6 I breathed a sigh of relief when the all-clear sounded. My cousin, Hiromi, left for work at the military shoe factory in Fukushima-cho. Michiko, my youngest sister, who normally would have been setting off for the munitions factory where she worked, had gone out to do labor service in the neighborhood, since she had the day off. My grandfather was a religious man and went to the Buddhist temple as he did every morning, carrying my one-year-old on his back and holding my two-year-old twins by the hand. My three- and four-year-old daughters, Etsuko and Tamiko, who had been playing in the garden, attached themselves to him and scampered off.

Thus only my sister Hisako and I were left at home. I had been about to use the toilet as the all-clear sounded, but my sister had gone in before me. I entered a few minutes later, just as the bomb fell. Because of my partial deafness, I did not hear anything. Suddenly I found the house collapsed around me and myself trapped in the lavatory. Perhaps irrationally, I cried out for help over and over again, and finally a man broke the door in and pulled me out.

Looking around for my sister, I saw her lying sprawled in the corridor, the right side of her body covered with terrible burns. She had probably been washing her hands, with her right hand stretched over the washbasin, when caught by the searing heat. I put my sister on my back and fled barefoot to Hijiyama Park. Her face was festering from her burns, and her right eye was hanging out. I pushed the eye back into its socket and tried to use a gauze mask to hold it in place, but her ear had melted away, and there was nothing to attach the mask to. Her mouth was twisted to the right, and she could do no more than whimper for water, only the first syllable of the word emerging distinctly.

On reaching Hijiyama Park, I laid my sister down on the ground and set off to search for my children. The fires were still burning fiercely. In a streetcar that had been burned bright red, surrounded by people already killed by the fire, I saw a woman still holding onto a strap and calling for help. The intense heat prevented me from approaching her, however; there was nothing I could do. To a man sitting on some stone steps I said, "Come on, let's get away from here," and pulled him up by the hand, but as I did so, the skin came away from his hand and he fell slowly to the ground. I could see his shadow imprinted clearly on the wall behind where he had been sitting. Many people called out to me for help or water. Unburned because of having been in the lavatory, I could only bring my hands together and apologize to the people I passed as I searched for some sign of my children.

As it turned out, none of those who had left that morning ever came home again—not my five children, my grandfather, my sister Michiko, or my cousin. Not a bone remained for me to find and treasure. Our house burned down, so that I had not even a photograph to remember them by. My sister Hisako drew her last breath four days later, on the evening of August 10, in agony from her massive injuries. I will never forget the expression on her face when I tried to give her a drop of water.

I was alone.

When the war ended on August 15, I wept to think that the surrender had not come just a few days earlier. My misery was compounded when I learned that my husband had been killed in battle in New Guinea. In a short while, I began suffering the physical effects of the atomic bombing—diarrhea, fever, and bleeding gums.

Even now I continue to have nightmares of my children crying out that their feet are burning. Did they really suffer like that? I had not even been able to give a cup of water to those who had called out to me for help. Was there ever suffering like theirs? However much I try to put these memories behind me, the cries continue to pursue me.

My own physical suffering continues. I remarried after the war, but physically I have gradually deteriorated and now can do no more than hobble around the house with a stick.

I detest the United States. I feel anger toward the Japanese government for its present policy of cooperation with a country that could inflict such suffering on another people. Listen to me, wherever you are! The suffering of those who experienced the atomic bombing continues even now, and the effects of the radiation are being passed on to their children and their children's children.

I beg that never again may nuclear weapons be inflicted on anyone, anywhere.

The Face of Another

Fumiko Nonaka

In 1945 I had been married for three years and was living in Hiroshima. On the morning of August 6 I was doing demolition work near Hijiyama Bridge. Just after eight o'clock the woman next to me called out, "Look, there's a B-29!" At the instant I looked up from under the brim of my straw hat, there was a piercing flash that bit into my face. I felt my body shrivel with a hiss like that of dried cuttlefish when you grill it. Then I was blown into the air and lost consciousness.

I do not know how long I lay there, but when I came to I saw people running about in confusion, their skin so burned and inflamed that they were beyond recognition. Following the crowd, I eventually reached my house, only to find that it had burned down. I was a wretched sight. The skin had burned off my arms and hung from my fingertips. The strong sunlight made the pain excruciating, so I tore off a large lotus leaf from a plant in a pond and put it over my head for protection. My shirt and work trousers had been burned off me, leaving me with only my white underwear and the belt from my trousers. Just as it was growing dark, I found myself at an aid station, I do not know where. My face was so swollen that I could not open my eyes, and I was unable to walk another step. After vomiting some yellow liquid, I was overcome by nausea and lay down where I was.

Three days later, on August 9, my husband's voice sounded in my ears. I recognized it but could not move. It had not been easy to find me, since my body was disfigured beyond all recognition. It was only by the ring on my finger that he knew me and called my name. My brother, who had come from Osaka to look for me, told me later that in the festering mess of my face it was impossible to tell where my eyes or nose were and that the cavities around my eyes were pools of yellow pus.

I was taken back to Osaka on a stretcher, but there even the doctor gave me up. Every day the burns festered more and more, and on my pulpy face and on the front of my arms and legs scabs like the crinkled black skin of a broiled sardine appeared. My mother and brother would remove the scabs with tweezers, wash the area with a saline solution, then bathe it with cooking oil.

It was a year before I could return to my husband in Hiroshima. However, because I had received the flash of the bomb directly in my face, I found that I could no longer recognize my face as my own. My eyebrows and lips had disappeared, and I had developed great black and red keloids that covered my face like a mask.

As the days passed, my husband found it more and more difficult to live with such a weak and disfigured wife. Eventually he fathered a child on a woman he worked with and started living with her. I could do nothing but put up with the situation. But the new relationship did not last long, and he begged me to let him come back and bring the child, a dear little boy. I would take the baby on my back to go to pick up the milk ration. It was not easy to do, since the keloids on my shoulders hurt badly, and it took a lot out of me. However, because I pitied the child I devoted all my strength to bringing him up.

In 1950, when the boy was three, we moved to Niigata Prefecture in northern Japan, where my husband found work as a high school music teacher. However, our happiness there was short lived. My husband ran off with a woman student, taking his son with him. Left alone, I had to find a way to support myself. With my disfigured face and weak arms and legs, the only work I could find was that of a day laborer. Working with pickax and shovel and carrying earth and stones was hard for me. If what I carried was too heavy, the keloids would burst and bleed. I tired easily and often collapsed from anemia. I needed blood transfusions if I was to stay alive. Because my daily wage was only ¥240, while a blood transfusion cost ¥500, it was very difficult to earn enough to keep going. My loneliness grew more and more intense.

My husband returned to Niigata with the boy. However, he could not get regular work, so I continued working. Winters there are bitter. As I made my way through the snow with my straw carrying basket, the little boy, enveloped in a plastic raincoat, plodded behind me. It was a hard time for us. In 1958, thinking that my husband might be forced to pull himself together if I were not around, I wrenched myself away from the boy and returned alone to Osaka, where I continued to work as a day laborer in the Nishinari district.

Because of my keloids I received recognition as an atomic bomb victim under the Atomic Bomb Medical Treatment Law. In 1969, when a counseling center for atomic bomb victims opened in Osaka, I was the first to register. But despite the mental comfort I gained, I could not forget that I had lost forever the face of my youth. Nor could I wipe away the anger I felt when children jeered at my injuries in the street.

I heard that my husband died in the Atomic Bomb Hospital in Hiroshima in 1965. I thought again of the days when we had been young, attractive, and happy together. I remembered the husband with an artist's sensitivity whom I had loved, who would bring his unopened pay envelope home to me each month. I could still hear his voice calling, "Fumiko, Fumiko," when he found me at last after three days of searching through the desolation of Hiroshima. The atomic bomb had ruined his life, too.

Even though my face had been burned, the injury had not reached my heart, and I continued to live spiritually, supported by the other women at the center. I also became involved in the peace movement, and in 1982 a book detailing my experiences was published.

I am now working as a counselor at the center. I have been able to give help concerning registration to more than thirty people who have been through the same kind of experience as I. Although keloids and wounds remain, medical benefits under the present Hibakusha Special Welfare Law stop when people no longer need treatment. This situation is deplorable. A pension scheme should be set up for the victims and a Hibakusha Aid Law providing national compensation enacted. Such a law, befitting a country that has undergone atomic attack, would add moral weight to the government's commitment to a ban on nuclear weapons throughout the world.

Fragile Lives

Machiyo Kurokawa

I am a victim of the atomic bombing of Hiroshima. At the time I was a sixteen-year-old student. I remember that the bomb fell just as the principal finished his morning address at assembly. Suddenly the windows shone brilliantly, and the next second everything went black. I had not the slightest idea what had happened. I think I lost consciousness for a short while, for when I came to, the building had collapsed around me. Light was streaming in at one place, and I crawled desperately toward that point, pushing aside the debris that surrounded my body with all my strength until finally I reached the outside.

One of my friends commented that I had blood on my face. As I pushed the hair away from my face, I felt pain for the first time. My hand was cut, probably by the fragments of glass embedded in my face. I had not realized until then that there was anything wrong with me. There was a hospital next to the school, and I set off in that direction. It was then that I discovered that I had quite a large cut on my left knee.

The hospital had suffered considerably more damage than our school. We were told that off-duty nurses were buried in the ruins of the nurses' quarters. Everyone who could move was asked to help dig them out. And so patients became laborers and assisted in the rescue work.

After a while I began to feel sick and returned to the school. I do not know how much time elapsed, but after a while I realized that someone was calling my name. I looked up to see a figure in front of me, burned over her entire body, with not a hair on her head. Her only clothing was the elastic band from her underpants, and on her back was what looked like a dirty kimono dragging on the ground. As I looked more carefully at this apparition that was calling my name, I saw that it was a friend of my younger sister's, a pretty, pink-cheeked child. It was impossible to reconcile yesterday's image with what I now saw before me.

That day the first-year and second-year students of the girls' secondary school and the middle school had been mobilized to assist with demolition work in the center of the city. That girl had been among them. She did not know what had happened but had come to tell us that many people had been killed or wounded. She asked me to take her to one of the teachers, but because her whole body was burned I dared not touch her. A stretcher was brought, but when we were laying her on it, she let out a terrible cry. I almost dropped her in fright but finally put her down safely, urging her to bear up. Her flesh had disintegrated and flaked off when I touched her leg, exposing the bone. I cannot imagine how she had managed to walk as far as she had in that condition. She pleaded with us to go and help her friends, and one of the teachers immediately set off at a run, asking those who could face the possibility of death to follow him. We followed as best we could, but wherever we went fires were burning fiercely and there were long lines of people covered with burns.

Our school became a temporary hospital, the desks and floors covered with people. When night fell, the flames from the burning city were so bright we could read a newspaper in the classroom. We heard the drone of a B-29 approaching, and the sound made people cry out in fear for their mothers and cringe at the thought of another bomb. People died from sheer fear. It was probably an American reconnaissance plane taking the photographs and films of the damage that we see now. Whatever it was, it caused even more people to die of fright. When I see those photographs and films, I cannot suppress my anger; I wish I could ask the American authorities why they took pictures of those who had suffered so much already.

Our suffering did not end there. The Japanese military did not give us one word of warning that it was an atomic bomb that had been dropped and that the area around the hypocenter was dangerously radioactive. The Occupation forces sent the Atomic Bomb Casualty Commission to Hiroshima to examine many of the atomic bomb victims, but this was nothing but an investigation; no treatment was provided. Not only that; we were not told that many of our symptoms, such as bloody stools and bleeding noses and throats, were caused by radiation. For a long time afterward, we were hated and feared by those around us.

Later I went to Tokyo to go to school, but when I searched for lodgings, just saying I was from Hiroshima was enough for me to be refused point-blank any number of times. One time my room deposit was returned to me, with the excuse that the room had long since been promised to someone else. It is impossible to forget the sadness and bitterness I suffered then. I was not disfigured by large keloids, but my cuts had festered, and my back was scarred. When I went to a public bath, I was told not to come again. Since I had been more than three kilometers from the hypocenter at the time of the blast, I had suffered comparatively little, but even I had to cope with a number of such experiences.

In the wake of the Bikini incident of March 1954, when the crew of the Japanese fishing boat *Lucky Dragon V* was exposed to fallout from a U.S. thermonuclear test, the movement for the abolition of nuclear bombs began to gain massive support throughout Japan. We victims decided that we had to do something ourselves to improve our lives and formed the Japan Confederation of A- and H-Bomb Sufferers Organizations in 1956. In the years since then we have appealed to the Japanese government to acknowledge responsibility for the war and for its long neglect of the victims of Hiroshima and Nagasaki. We have

also pressed continuously for a Hibakusha Aid Law providing
state compensation for atomic bomb victims; this would be seen
as an expression of the government's resolve never to allow such
a thing to happen again.

In 1979 I was invited by a Dutch peace movement to speak of
my experiences and relate how victims have gone about their
lives. Since then I have been to Australia, New Zealand, Den-
mark, Sweden, and Italy, appealing to the people of the world.

For decades we have lived as victims of the bombing, decades
filled with inexpressible pain and anxiety. For a while I was in
and out of hospital so often that I kept a packed bag ready, not
knowing when I would need it. When I had not been hospitalized for a year or two, I felt great relief. Recently one morning,
however, I suddenly fell ill again, and by evening I had almost
lost consciousness and found myself in hospital again. An atomic
bomb victim has to live with the realization that he or she is a
broken person. Even after exhaustive tests, we still do not know
what is wrong with us. The doctors themselves say there is
something in the bodies of atomic bomb victims that is beyond
their understanding. Though prey to constant anxiety, we have
to continue living somehow.

However fragile they may be, our lives are precious. We must
make our suffering and our anxiety known while we still live.

Four Days of Hiroshima

Hiroshi Shibayama

At 7:50 on the morning of August 6 I left the house of the Nishiokas, with whom I was staying, in the Hiratsuka-cho district of Hiroshima west of Hijiyama Park, and set off with their son for the industrial machinery factory of the Hiroshima Railway office in the suburb of Yaga. I was twenty at the time. My company in Kuwana, near Nagoya, had sent me to Hiroshima in connection with supplying steam engine boilers to the factory.

It was about 1.3 kilometers to Hiroshima Station. On the way, as usual, we heard an air-raid alert but did not take much notice of it. In the clear blue sky the midsummer sun was beginning to make itself felt, and the people commuting to work or school seemed to be in the best of spirits. Arriving at the station, we raced to make our train. At that moment the line between my life and death was drawn. It was about two kilometers to my destination, some five minutes' travel. I stood in the open area of the railway car and savored the fresh air. Arriving at Yaga Station, we hurried to the factory along a narrow lane bordered by a high brick wall.

Suddenly I heard the sharp crack of an explosion. I stumbled forward, then fell sideways. My hat blew off. The wall of the factory collapsed in a pile of dust. What had happened? Without thinking I turned around to look in the direction of the explosion. The Nishioka boy cried out, "How beautiful!" Rising rapidly into the cobalt blue sky was a towering mass of cloud—deep red, yellow, white, blue, purple, all the colors swirling violently. Unaware of its import, I was fascinated by its beauty.

The force of the explosion had ripped the tiles from the roofs of the houses all around, and the shattered glass of the factory roof fell on us like rain. At first we thought that a powder magazine had exploded, but the sight of that enormous mushroom-shaped cloud forced us to conclude that something monstrous had happened. I remember that the expressions on our faces hardened.

Without making any conscious decision, we both started running back in the direction of the city. My head was pounding with blood. It was two and a half kilometers to Hiratsuka-cho as the crow flies. Though only my temporary residence, for the Nishioka boy it was his whole family, his home.

When we had gone about one kilometer, we were brought to a standstill by a grotesque group of people. The blood pounded in our heads again. I remember that my eyes were drawn inexorably to the scene. The people were burned so badly that it was hard to distinguish feature from feature, and all were blackened, as if covered with soot. Their clothes were in rags; many were naked. Their hands hung limply in front of them. The skin of their hands and arms dangled from their fingertips. Their faces were not the faces of the living. I grasped Nishioka's hand, unable to believe what I saw.

I had been in a number of air raids. During the great air raid of March on Nagoya a one-ton bomb had fallen on the Aichi Clock factory, a four-story ferroconcrete building, and had penetrated to the ground floor. When it exploded, the people in the building were reduced to thousands of pieces of meat splattered on the surrounding walls. I had been there immediately after.

Another unforgettable incident occurred during the fire bombing of Kuwana, when a single bomb, while still falling, broke into scores of smaller incendiary bombs that fell like a rain of fire. A fragment hit the head of an air-raid warden, tearing off a piece of his skull. Crying out in pain, he tumbled into a barrel of water kept for fighting fires, staining the water with his blood as he died. I had sustained myself with the thought that this, after all, was war.

How could I comprehend what I saw before me now? It was not just a group of injured people. Nor was it a procession of the dead or a band of ghosts. No sound came from these figures; they seemed to have given up. The pity they engendered is beyond expression. They continued to stream past in deathly quiet. How can anyone describe them—their clothes ripped from them by the force of the explosion, their bodies burned by the intense heat? Some were completely naked, and others had only their shirts stuck to their bodies. The injuries to their faces were particularly cruel. Unscathed and with clothes intact, I felt like an intruder. It was as if the normal and the abnormal had been reversed.

We set off again at a run, overtaking more lines of people stumbling in the opposite direction. Eventually we arrived at the bridge near Hiroshima Station over a tributary of the Kyobashi River. As we crossed, we were transfixed by the horror of what we saw below us in the river. It was like a painting of hell. Floating there were scores of dead bodies, faces swollen to twice their normal size and trouser-encased legs stiff as logs. The upper half of one body was burned black and the lower half swollen and waterlogged. The sight chilled us to the bone. We also saw the swollen carcasses of horses.

We ran on. Soon we came to Hiratsuka-cho, but now it was a sea of fire, and we could get nowhere near Nishioka's home. Only the eyes in Nishioka's pallid face seemed alive as he looked fixedly in the direction of his house, the home where his parents and grandparents had been born and had lived. He must have been laboring under a flood of emotions, wondering what had happened to his father, his mother, his younger sister. Unconsciously, he was gripping his hands tightly together.

Ashes and sparks from the black smoke and the flames were swirling around us. The heat was becoming too strong to bear, and with an exchange of looks that signaled our helplessness, we decided to retreat. Now we fled for our lives before the intensity of the fires. Our faces seemed to burn in the heat. Where or how we ran I have no recollection. We went along the road that skirted Hijiyama Park and led to Hiroshima Station. When we had come that way earlier, the station had been almost untouched; now it was enveloped in sheets of flame.

Not knowing what else to do, we decided to go back to the house of an acquaintance in Yaga. We joined the throngs of injured and refugees who were dispiritedly making their way toward the countryside. Where would they go? What would they do for food, for water? The faces of all were blackened, and most were suffering from burns on all the exposed parts of their bodies.

It began to rain. Black stains spotted shirts. The multicolored smoke generated at the time of the blast had become a cloud of dirty brown and black hanging like a pall over the city. It was a demonic ceiling, a malediction.

We were exhausted. Too tired even to talk, we eventually reached the house of our acquaintance and spent the night, sleeping in our clothes. Hiroshima was aflame and bright as day. In such a conflagration, there was nothing at all we could do either for the dead or for those suffering from injuries. Nor could we help the people we saw roaming about in search of loved ones. All we could do was steel ourselves and keep silent. It was more than a human being could bear.

As day broke, the heavy cloud turned a murky red but remained hanging in the sky. We decided that we had to go back into the city to search for Nishioka's parents and sister. We could only avert our eyes from the pitiful scenes that confronted us as we made our way into Hiroshima. As we approached the city center, things worsened immeasurably. One figure that we came across is engraved in my mind: a man, his face burned and his blue clothes in shreds, riding along apathetically with what looked like black wood fastened to his bicycle with coarse straw rope. As he approached, we saw that what we had taken for wood was a stiff, blackened corpse, probably the remains of a loved one. The man himself seemed crazed. All the inhabitants of Hiroshima appeared deranged. We too, as we stumbled over charred corpses, felt nothing more than if they had been rocks.

We knew that Nishioka's sister, a student at the Hiroshima Girls' Commercial School, had been scheduled to take part in demolition work as part of the school's contribution to the war effort. We made contact with the school and then set out for the site where she would have been working. After several hours of searching, we finally came across a clue to her whereabouts. In the auditorium of a school near Hijiyama Park we found about two hundred injured schoolgirls lying in rows on the tatami-matted floor. It was a cruel sight. Most of them, clad only in the gym clothes that they had worn to the demolition site, white blouses and black bloomers, had suffered burns. Some of them wore only blouses, their bloomers having been burned off them. Their skin was in shreds, hanging loosely from their bodies, and most of them were burned black. Their cries of pain, their whimpers for water or their mothers, turned the scene into a living hell.

We went around, looking into the face of each girl and questioning those who could respond, and eventually found Nishioka's sister. Her burns seemed to be comparatively light, which visibly relieved her brother. She was crying, but when she had regained her composure a little, she asked worriedly after their parents.

There seemed to be only one doctor and two nurses, aided by a policeman and some people who appeared to be relatives of the victims, looking after all the injured people there. The policeman came over to us and asked us if we were well. "You can see that we don't have enough people to help look after all the injured here. Please stay and lend a hand." It was half an order. We did not really want to stay but in view of the situation could do nothing else. Thus we turned to nursing the injured. There was no medicine, gauze, or bandages. All we had was some olive oil and ointment. Even the doctor was confined to disinfecting wounds. We passed the night keenly aware of our helplessness.

The third day dawned. The cries for water and loved ones continued unabated, and many people breathed their last. We brought our palms together before them and whispered a prayer in our hearts.

The doctor had strictly forbidden the patients to be given water, but I took it on myself to pour water from the spout of a kettle into their open mouths. It was just like pouring water into the vases on graves. Their features took on the semblance of a smile as they murmured their thanks. The water would probably contribute to the formation of pus and thus hasten death, but I looked on it as the parting cup. Stubbornly, I continued to give a little water to each person. I was well aware that their ease might be only momentary, but I told myself that it was probably the last joy they were to have in this world.

Eventually we had no tears left. In the merciless summer heat I felt my body becoming more and more languid. Still, I pulled myself together and went on wiping the pus from wounds. It was about this time that the festering became severe. It was the face that was particularly affected, puffed up like a full moon, so that we could not look directly at the sufferer. It was also then that I noticed another patient. Amid the pus welling from the eyes and the nose was something white and moving. Looking more closely, I was horrified to see maggots. Surely the person had died? But no, breath remained! What was this? Could maggots breed in living bodies? Making my mind a blank, I wiped the maggots away, only to find the same thing again with the next person.

Can you, in this time of peace, really believe these things? Can you understand just how different those flash burns from the atomic bomb were from ordinary burns? People continued to die. Try to comprehend our feelings as we had to let that happen, unable to do anything for the victims. Can you imagine the living hell it was? It is impossible for me to write any more about it. Forgive me. Sometimes scenes from that time flash vivivdly into my mind, and I cannot hold back my tears.

Thus passed the third day. The next morning I decided to return to my company in Kuwana and had the policeman write

me a note as proof that I had been detained by the disaster. I
guessed that trains would be running from a station about five
kilometers away and set off in that direction. Around this time
military and civilian relief teams were entering the city in large
numbers.

On August 14 I was back in Hiroshima. The following day I
went to the factory to help reopen it. I found the place astir and
all the employees gathered in the open area in front. I was told
that the Emperor was to make a radio broadcast at noon. We
expected that he was going to encourage us to a last defense of
the main islands, but the address turned out to be a declaration
that the war was over.

Everyone was in tears. This development was particularly
ironic, coming immediately after the tragedy that Hiroshima
had just suffered. Regret and indignation flooded my body, followed by a stupor of blank amazement. What was the best
thing to do in the circumstances? Soon after, I suddenly felt an
overwhelming fatigue and fever and realized something was
wrong with me.

I decided to return as quickly as possible to my home in
Kyoto. I pushed myself aboard the packed train and slid under a
seat. In my extreme fatigue, at some point I fell asleep. When I
arrived at Kyoto Station, I could hardly propel myself along
the walkways and staircases. I remember how slowly the time
seemed to pass. As I went out of the wicket, though, I felt my
birthplace draw me into its embrace.

The next day I went to my doctor and was immediately sent to
the public hospital for emergency treatment. Blood tests showed
a drop in my white cell count, and the doctors were worried. It
was then that I realized how close I was to death. For several
days test followed test, including a series of harrowing tests that
revealed that radiation had affected the bone marrow.

I was given the best treatment possible at a time when medical
supplies were scarce, and that, together with injections and
transfusions of blood from my brothers—who lost weight as a
result—restored me to health in three months. I am grateful to
all concerned that I am able to live an active life today.

The Real Victims

Katsuo Fukushima

I used to have a bookshop in the Ise-machi district of Nagasaki. On August 9, 1945, I had business in another part of town, and so it was that I was riding my bicycle near Sakura-machi when a B-29 flew over and dropped an atomic bomb. Luckily, my wife and three-year-old daughter were able to take refuge in an air-raid trench after our house was destroyed and thus were saved, but my wife's left shoulder was seriously injured. I was badly hurt, too, but despite my injuries I set out the next day for the center of the city to search for relatives and friends. There I spent four or five days.

In 1946 my eyesight began to deteriorate and eventually became so bad that I was unable to work. Since I had been told I could find a good doctor in Tokyo, I moved there in 1952. Meanwhile, I started to have trouble with my respiratory tract, and for the next twenty years I could not sleep at night if I did not go to the hospital for a daily injection. I also suffered hearing loss.

For the past four or five years I have experienced sudden bleeding from the right ear. Our local ear, nose, and throat specialist advised me to seek treatment at a large hospital, and I went to the Azukizawa Hospital in Itabashi Ward. There a doctor from Nihon University told me that the problem, if not treated, could lead to meningitis and affect the brain. Because I was an atomic bomb victim and elderly, extensive surgery was impossible, and only some affected parts could be excised.

At present I am receiving treatment at the Oyama Geriatric Hospital and am taking three kinds of medicine, including antibiotics. Because of my hearing loss, I have followed the doctors' advice to wear a hearing aid and am now able to carry on a conversation.

The frightful suffering that occurred in the second the atomic bomb exploded is beyond imagination and can only be suggested by some of the medieval paintings of hell. Here in Tokyo about a hundred thousand people died in the massive air raids, and the sufferings of the many more who were injured were pitiful. The plight of those repatriated after the war was also often desperate. Altogether over three million precious lives were lost in the war. More than three hundred thousand people died in Hiroshima and Nagasaki alone, the world's first victims of nuclear holocaust.

The hell that we survived will last as long as we continue to fall victim to its aftereffects, specifically, radiation-induced disorders. Many of those who experienced the atomic bombings have been bedridden for decades and can do nothing but wait for death. Even those who look no different from the people around them live in constant fear that someday the dreaded symptoms will appear. They also tire much more easily than normal people. In Itabashi, where I live, there is a person who has spent nearly forty years alone, unable to marry because of disfiguring keloids on the face, shoulders, and arms.

Another case in Itabashi concerns a woman who applied for a job preparing school lunches. The ward office rejected her application because she was an atomic bomb victim. It was only after strong protests to the ward office by our supporters, people from the peace movement, and others of good will that she was allowed to take on the job.

When I applied for Post Office Life Insurance, my application was initially accepted, only to be turned down by the head office, also because I was an atomic bomb victim. Thus, we face discrimination even from the government.

For more than twenty years I have taken an active part in the antinuclear movement. When my daughter reached adulthood, she said to me, "I think what you are doing is wonderful and absolutely right. But I have a problem. People from the media come to interview you and take your picture and you also appear on TV. I can't stand the pressure any longer and want to leave home." So saying, she turned her back on me and went to live alone.

When I speak about the atomic bomb, people often tell me that they went through the Tokyo air raids, losing their homes and loved ones. I know that the war brought pain and suffering to many, but they are able to talk about it quite nonchalantly now. Few survivors of Hiroshima and Nagasaki, however, are willing to admit publicly that they were victims of the atomic bomb. If they do so, they are likely to find marriage impossible and employment hard to find, since prospective spouses and employers worry about the possible onset of debilitating disorders caused by exposure to radiation.

Nuclear weapons are now being stockpiled in vast quantities. There is no way of knowing where and when they may be exploded. The problem of the deployment of neutron bombs in Europe and similar questions have involved people as never before in the movement to ban nuclear arms.

This is the meaning of the plea of the atomic bomb victims over many years for the enactment of a Hibakusha Aid Law. The Conference on Fundamental Problems of Measures for the Victims of the Atomic Bombs, sponsored by the Japanese government, has submitted a report opposing enactment of such a law. According to the report, suffering caused by war is to be shared equally. In other words, everyone must share in the suffering.

Who causes war? It is the government in power at the time. Ordinary citizens are always sacrificed. We do not feel that a Hibakusha Aid Law would really be enough for atomic bomb victims. We are not spurred by the thought of a solatium for bereaved families. Our reason for demanding that the government enact such a law is to make it prove that it is truly willing to ban nuclear weapons and work for peace, rejecting war as a solution to international disputes.

My wife is also an atomic bomb victim. She is physically weak and has been in and out of hospital for many years. Our family has been destroyed. I pray that what we have experienced will not happen again and that a third nuclear weapon will never be exploded in war anywhere in the world.

My Pilgrimage

Masae Kawai

Both my husband and I are survivors of the atomic bombing of Hiroshima. I had been mobilized to work in the accounting section of the headquarters of the army marine division in the Ujina district, about four and a half kilometers from the hypocenter. On the morning of August 6, following the sounding of the all-clear, we were in the grounds exercising with bamboo spears.

Suddenly there was a great cracking sound. So great was the ringing in my ears that I could hear nothing for a few seconds. Looking in the direction of the noise, I saw a vast cloud shaped like a mushroom rising into the sky—the notorious cloud formation of the atomic bomb. Our stupefaction broken by the command to take cover, we all leaped into the air-raid trenches. Every pane of glass in the building had been shattered by the force of the explosion, and the floor was covered with broken glass and scattered documents.

Our uneasiness was compounded by not knowing whether the explosion had been caused by a delayed-action bomb or some totally new and unknown weapon. As the city started to burn, we grew aware of an unearthly procession trailing toward Ujina. It was composed of people smeared with ash and blood, some

with their clothes in rags around them and others completely naked, their hands flopping uselessly in front of them. Adults and
children alike were crying. They looked like evacuees from hell.
Now and again a figure would fall with a thud in the midst of the
shuffling mass, crying out for help or water.

We worked frantically to carry people to the ferries that would
take them from the port to the hospital on the island of Nino-
shima, and before I realized it, my hands and clothes were covered with blood. When the boats were full, we laid people down
on the concrete in the open area nearby, and soon there were so
many that there was scarcely space to walk between the bodies.
We would have liked to put them indoors, but the buildings
were already packed. Most of the people were suffering from
injuries and massive burns and were whimpering for water. We
had been told that to give water to the badly burned would only
hasten death. All we could do was try to ease their suffering by
cooling their burns with towels moistened in cold water. We had
to watch as the sufferers' breathing grew fainter and they died
one by one.

The center of the city glowed red as the fires took hold. We
could do nothing but wait helplessly, not knowing the fate of our
families there. The next day, wanting to know what had happened to my home and to find out if my mother and sister were
all right, I found a ride in an army truck and managed to reach
the vicinity of our house. Although it was about three kilometers
from the center of the city, the house had been destroyed and
there was no sign of my family.

As I stood there feeling dazed, I suddenly realized that an apparition was calling my name. Its clothes were in soiled tatters;
its face was swathed in gauze with holes left for the eyes, nose,
and mouth. A bandage was wrapped around its head, and it
limply held out two hands swollen to twice their normal size by
burns. Even now the ghastliness of that scene strikes a chill to
my heart.

"Masae, don't you know your mother?" asked the voice. My
mother! She told me that she had gone to the Hakushima district
to send off soldiers, that she had been badly burned, and that she

had just now got back. "And look what's happened to me," she cried out, starting to weep. She then began to fear for the safety of my younger sister, a first-year student at the girls' secondary school who had been clearing the sites of demolished houses near what is now Peace Memorial Park—the hypocenter. That morning my sister had not been feeling well, and since she was not strong, my mother had told her to rest. Apparently she had got up, however, packed herself a lunch, dressed herself in some of my work clothes, and set off without telling anyone.

My father was in China, and my mother was badly burned. If I did not do something, who would? I set off at once into the city to search but could not get close to the city center because of the blaze. The next day I tried again and, choking with the smoke and heat, forced my way through burned corpses into the city center. There I saw people who were no more than sticks of charcoal, others who had died as they piled on top of one another seeking relief in the troughs of water kept to fight fires. I spent the entire day going from corpse to corpse, checking to see whether my sister was among them. Bodies were floating in the rivers; when I drew some near with a pole, others would bob up from below. All the faces were bloated and swollen from their immersion; the skin of their heels resembled layers of pie crust, swollen and waving in the water. I was so desperate to find my sister that I felt no nausea or fear.

The smell of the charred bodies was overpowering. In the hot midsummer sun, bubbles of blood welled out of the eyes, ears, noses, and mouths of the corpses. Their lips were three times normal size. In the corridors and gardens of the Red Cross Hospital lay masses of patients who could not be accommodated in beds, groaning in pain. Their wounds were infested with flies, and maggots had begun to breed. As night fell, we could see the smoke and smell the stench of bodies being cremated on the river banks and in the open spaces near the houses. The burning phosphorus made will-o'-the-wisps fly about.

Since most of the dead were either naked or covered only with tatters of clothing, all I had to go by in my search for my sister was the small amount of material that usually remained attached to the elastic waistband of the baggy work trousers we all wore. I continued my pilgrimage through the city, examining each remnant of cloth I came across. But I never found anything that I could identify as belonging to her.

During my wanderings I found myself stricken suddenly with a high fever and began to suffer from diarrhea and severe vomiting. My mouth became badly ulcerated, and my gums started bleeding. I had no appetite. I found myself a seat in a bicycle-driven cart and had myself taken to Ujina for treatment. A theory was going around that if one's hair began to fall out, there was little chance of survival. The people caring for me were very apprehensive, but fortunately my hair did not fall out. Within two weeks my temperature dropped, but my whole body turned yellow. It was diagnosed as nothing worse than jaundice. I had escaped death. When I could walk again, I set off once more in search of my sister.

I nursed the hope that she might have been taken to one of the relief centers in the Inland Sea, and I took the ferry from island to island, checking the registration books of the various facilities. Since almost all the patients had already died, I described her to the nurses and went through the books. On Taibi Island, my heart leaped when I found her name registered at the relief center. However, it turned out that the patient, who had already died, had been a middle-aged woman with the same name. I have never heard of anyone coming to claim her remains. Perhaps her whole family died in the blast.

I was never to find any trace of my sister. Even now I cannot stop the tears from flowing when I see someone who looks like her. I cry whenever I meet my cousin, who is the same age. Each year, as August 6 approaches, the newspapers and television are full of reports about the atomic bomb. It hurts to remember the brutality, and I turn off the television and refuse to look at the newspapers. I live in fear of the outbreak of radiation-related disorders. I ask myself every day when they are going to strike. My husband and I, both victims, bearing the same wounds, never speak of the bomb if we can help it; we live quietly, doing our best to put it from our minds. We never talk to others about it. Even if we could, the hideousness of the experience is beyond the power of words to describe. Nevertheless, things continue to happen that do not permit us to forget.

After I married and moved to Tokyo, I began to suffer from anemia, nausea, and bad mouth ulcers. When my son was six and my daughter four, I was hospitalized for four months because of anemia and an abnormal white cell count. I had to have blood transfusions every day, buying blood from those who came to sell it. The expense was a great burden. After a month I began to itch unbearably over my entire body. The doctors stopped the transfusions and instead injected nutrients directly into my breastbone. Pain and anxiety were my constant companions. When I look back on that time, I cannot help feeling that I had a great deal of endurance.

Despite all my treatment, I had to return home without any substantial improvement, and my anxiety about my health became a neurosis. I pestered my husband with my fear of dying. Just getting on a bus can bring on a wave of nausea, and in the morning when I clean my teeth, my gums bleed and I feel like vomiting. As always, my mouth ulcerates easily, and when this happens I can neither eat nor talk. I tire easily and am plagued by lack of energy. Those who do not know what is wrong with me put my problem down to laziness. In the evening I tend to get headaches, and my eyes grow so tired that I can hardly keep them open. I struggle constantly with ill health.

Six years ago I was hospitalized again. My trouble was diagnosed as a liver ailment brought on by my exposure to radiation and by tranfusions of bad blood, and incurable because of chronic hepatitis and a fatty liver. I was ordered to get plenty of sleep and never to overexert myself if I did not want the condition to worsen. Once every two months I have to have a blood test. I also go regularly to an osteopath for electrical treatment to prevent cumulative fatigue. When I think about the future, particularly now that I am growing older, I am filled with anxiety.

My mother is still alive in Hiroshima, also passing her days apprehensively. I pray that a Hibakusha Aid Law for atomic bomb victims will be enacted in her lifetime.

A Survivor's Responsibility

Sumiteru Taniguchi

I was sixteen years old at the time—11:02 on the morning of August 9, 1945, three days after the atomic bombing of Hiroshima. I was delivering mail, riding my bicycle near the Mitsubishi Armaments factory, when an atomic bomb was dropped about a kilometer and a half away. The wind from the blast, coming from behind, hurled me and my bicycle to the ground. A brilliant light momentarily dazzled me, and I cowered face down on the road. When I looked up, I saw that a little child who had been playing nearby was being tossed about like a leaf. Then stones thirty centimeters in diameter came flying through the air, hitting me and bouncing off.

As I felt the ground move beneath me like an earthquake, I thought that a bomb must have fallen very close by. I wondered if I was fated to die then and there but clutched desperately to the heartening fact that I was still alive. A great hatred for the war that let such things happen overwhelmed me, and I was filled with bitter resentment toward the adults who had done nothing to try to prevent it. The same thought was to recur over and over during the long period of pain and suffering to follow.

I think two or three minutes passed before the earth stopped trembling and I heaved myself up. My bicycle was twisted like soft toffee. The skin of my left arm had peeled from the upper arm to the tips of my fingers and was hanging in strips. When I felt my back and buttocks, I found that the skin there had been burned to a pulp and that only the front part of the clothes I had been wearing remained. Strangely enough, there was absolutely no blood, and I felt no pain at all. I was totally numb mentally, too, unable to absorb the suffering I saw around me. When I thought about it later, I surmised that I must have been momentarily paralyzed by the shock and suffered a kind of blackout, though at first I thought I had remained conscious throughout the period.

Around me fire was spurting from houses. Only the house where I had just delivered mail still stood, almost untouched. The child who had been blown about was dead, without a sign of injury. My hat had been whisked away somewhere. I gathered together the scattered mail and stuffed it back into the bag, placing it beside my bicycle. Then I began to walk toward the hills. On the way I passed the ruins of the women's dormitory at the Mitsubishi plant. It was full of injured people, most with their hair so burned that it was impossible to tell men from women.

Here and there on the nearby hills trees were burning. Eventually I made my way to a Mitsubishi factory, some five hundred meters distant, that had been dug out of a small hill. I sat down on a bench at the entrance and asked some men who were there to cut off the strips of skin hanging from my left arm. In place of ointment, they smeared my burns with machine oil and told me that the area would not be safe for long. I tried to leave but found that my legs would not support me. One of the workers carried me up to the top of the hill on his back. That was the beginning of my long period of immobility.

In the hills there was neither food nor drink. Rain began to fall during the night, and we collected the droplets from the bamboo leaves to ease our parched throats. The fires of Nagasaki spread in every direction, and the flames stained the sky. American planes flew over fairly often, strafing the fleeing people. Occasionally stray bullets struck the rocks near where I was sleeping, and their noise added to the unearthly quality of the place. It was a night of pain and anxiety.

I spent two nights in the hills together with a large number of corpses. On the third day a relief team found me and put me on a train for Isahaya, twenty-eight kilometers from Nagasaki. There I was accommodated in a primary school, without, however, any medical attention worthy of the name. On my second day there, when I was taken out of bed to go to the toilet, I was suddenly attacked by searing pain and started hemorrhaging.

On August 15, the day the war ended, I was moved to the primary school in the village of Nagayo, where I had relatives, but no treatment was available there, either. In the middle of September I heard that doctors from Nagasaki Medical College were offering treatment at the Shinkozen Primary School in Nagasaki, and I was taken the twelve or thirteen kilometers there by cart. At long last I had proper medical supervision. I was given blood transfusions but could only take about twenty milliliters at a time and so was unable to respond to the careful treatment. In November I was transferred to the navy hospital in Omura.

When I saw the bright fruit of the persimmon tree outside my window I became nostalgic for the carefree days of my childhood and could not help feeling sad that such happiness might never come my way again. As the days passed, there was no sign of my wounds healing; the pain was actually growing worse. When I heard the sound of the gurney coming to take me for treatment, I would whimper and beg them to let me die. As if the burns on my back were not enough, I was also suffering from bad bedsores from having to lie on my stomach all the time.

In March 1946 the food stuck in my throat; and in September, phlegm that I could not get rid of by myself clogged my throat and even stopped my breathing for a time. The skin of my half-burned body began to fester and ooze pus, which flowed onto the bedding. Soaked in a sea of pus, I begged time and time again to be allowed to die. The smell of rotting bodies and burned flesh, and the pain of maggots in living flesh, were the accompaniments of each weird day.

At the end of October 1946 I was given a new medicine. After taking it for five or six days, I began to feel much more comfortable, the pain of my wounds subsided, and I could see for myself that I was finally getting better. It was then, for the first time, that I asked for a mirror to be brought to me so that I could look at my wounds.

In May 1947, after a year and nine months, I was able to lower my legs to the ground unassisted. I was eighteen by that time. My joy knew no bounds. I had returned to life. I had actually endured the experience. I still remember how happy the doctors, the nurses, and the other patients were when I began to walk again, as if a baby were taking its first steps.

My injuries covered the outer part of my left arm, my back, my buttocks, the upper part of my right arm, the outer part of my left thigh, and the back of my head. The left side of my face, my chin, my chest, and both knees were scarred from bedsores. I could not extend my left arm at the elbow more than 110 degrees, so in 1948 I had an operation to graft skin to it from my right thigh. The operation was not a total success, however; though the graft took, a keloid formed.

The wound on my back did not improve; even so, I was told I could leave the hospital in March 1948. But then a new kind of suffering and anxiety began. Could I work with others on an equal footing? How would people look on me? Overcome by fears, each evening I would go outside and weep. When it was time for me to be discharged, I had to borrow my brother's clothes, having none of my own. I recall as if it were yesterday the doctors and nurses, along with my roommates, waving goodbye until they were lost in the distance.

I returned to my job in the post office in April that year. Many of my former co-workers had been lost near the hypocenter on August 9, 1945. There were also a number with injuries who had returned to work but later died. It seemed a miracle that I, with the most serious injuries of all, should have survived. I drove my easily tired body, vowing to work every bit as hard as my co-workers.

The Bikini hydrogen bomb test in March 1954 came as a great

shock to us. The following year, as a result of popular feeling, the first World Conference Against Atomic and Hydrogen Bombs was held in Hiroshima. Nagasaki hosted the second conference in 1956. I was a member of one of the subcommittees, where for the first time I spoke of my experiences as an atomic bomb victim. From that time on, I grew more and more convinced that I should participate in workers' unions and peace movements. My co-workers saw this as natural and gave me their support. I think they realized that what I was doing had an inherent honesty born of my cruel experiences.

I underwent plastic surgery on my face at the Nagasaki University Hospital in 1956, but my back injury failed to improve. I could not stand the thought of a series of operations, but finally, in 1960, I had the scar removed under general anesthetic at the Atomic Bomb Hospital in Hiroshima and skin grafted onto the spot. Even so, more than half my body is scarred. In the summer my back, deprived of sweat glands, aches with a dull, unrelieved pain. Blisters form where there are keloids. In winter, just like an old person, I cannot retain body warmth. Moreover, if I gain much weight, my wounds ache as if about to burst open, so I eat only enough to keep me going from day to day.

An invitation to go to East Germany for treatment came in 1961, and I went, hoping that a successful operation could be performed on my left elbow. However, after I was examined I was told that a major operation would be impossible because of a chronic blood disorder, and I went home disappointed.

Returning to work and continuing treatment for my symptoms, I began to look for a wife. Time and time again I was refused. "How could you imagine that I would marry someone with your injuries? You can't even look forward to a long life!" I heard that over and over again.

Eventually a marriage was arranged through the good offices of my aunt. Before our marriage my wife evidently was told only of the injuries to my face. Not till our honeymoon did she see the scars on my body, and after that she could not stop crying. When we returned together, everyone seemed amazed. I had no idea why; when I asked, I was told that no one thought the two of us would come back together. I heard later that my wife was inclined at first to accuse my aunt of hiding the truth from her but soon began to think that if she did not take on the responsibility of looking after me, no one else would.

When my wife became pregnant with our first child, we both worried about producing a normal baby. Luckily, it was perfectly normal, and we felt great relief. Other problems arose, however. For example, in summer when we went to the beach, I felt embarrassed to take off my shirt in front of others and would keep it on even while swimming. Later, emboldened by the antinuclear movement, I plucked up my courage and exposed my back, thinking that people who saw it might be inspired to join the movement themselves. My wife fully supported me in this and in my activities for the peace movement. My children also put aside their personal feelings and appeared to understand my urgent need to bear witness to what had happened. Gradually I learned to feel joy in living despite my pain and suffering. In living, I could fight death. I felt great satisfaction that I had been able to fight both the war and the atomic bomb.

At the antibomb conference in Hiroshima in 1955, Misako Yamaguchi and Yukie Tsuji, young women whose youth was destroyed by the war and the atomic bomb, spoke for the first time before a large audience of the reality of the bomb and the suffering it had caused. Their tearful appeals earned them the sympathy and understanding of all present. That encouraged us to form an association in Nagasaki of forty or fifty young men and women who had experienced the atomic bombing, and we decided to campaign for world peace so that such suffering might never be repeated. Unless we bomb victims ourselves tell what really happened, how can others know the suffering engendered by war and the horrors of the atomic bomb? It is our responsibility to gather our courage and bear witness to what we experienced. We resolved that this should be our purpose in life.

Today, the people in the association are well into their fifties. It retains its original name, however, the Association of Nagasaki Youths, to recall our initial vow. We continue to fight as a member group of the antinuclear movement and the organization of bomb victims in Nagasaki.

Though that nightmarish day is now far in the past, many people die every year from diseases linked to the bomb. I am aware that if I fall victim to such a disease, all I can do is wait for death. Nevertheless, while I live I will devote myself to the well-being of all people everywhere.

One of my close friends committed suicide in the summer of 1957 as August was approaching, saying that he could not bear to hear the word *August* on people's lips. When August 9 comes, I still cannot forget that day of living hell. I remember it as if it were yesterday as I relive the pain and suffering.

People around the world have different-colored skin and hair and eyes, but the color of the blood in their veins is the same. We will never meet or talk to, much less grow to hate, the vast majority of these people. Why, and for whose benefit, are we then compelled to kill one another? If we ourselves do not protect the culture and civilization that we create and inherit, who will do it for us? Weapons can only kill and destroy; they cannot protect and create.

For decades now we atomic bomb victims have been appealing to the people of the world for nuclear disarmament. But the countries possessing nuclear arms continue to produce and test them. They dupe their citizens with the myth of nuclear deterrence. While we survivors of the atomic bombing live, we will campaign resolutely, with the help of people of good will everywhere, for the banning of nuclear weapons from the face of the earth and for an end to war, so that our children may inhabit a world of peace. As a parent, I will continue to strive in the hope that I may witness such a time with my own eyes, exerting all my strength to further the antinuclear and peace movements and to aid the atomic bomb victims, as well as people everywhere.

The Unknown Victims

Lee Gi-sang

I find it difficult to talk about a good part of my life. Being Korean, I cannot divorce myself from the suffering of my compatriots, and I am ripped apart by my memories. Because of Japanese militarism, I was pushed into forced labor and made to suffer countless instances of discrimination and oppression, finally becoming a victim of the atomic bomb. Fate decreed that I be coerced into sacrificing my body and blood "for the sake of the Emperor."

I was born into a poor farming family in South Cholla Province. As the oldest of six children, I wanted to become self-supporting as early as possible so that I could add my share to the family's finances. Thus when I was seventeen I made my way to Japan and worked in factories and on construction sites around Osaka. As the years went by, the war in China expanded, to be followed by the outbreak of World War II. Soon after, I was drafted to work in the Kawanami Shipyard on the island of Koyagi, outside the port of Nagasaki.

In Nagasaki alone there were five or six thousand Koreans. Some of us had been mobilized in Japan for forced labor, while others had been brought over from Korea. We lived in barracks, sleeping on bare boards. At night we had only a single ragged

Akihiro Takahashi speaks at an international antinuclear rally in Hiroshima. Formerly direc-
tor of the Hiroshima Peace Memorial Museum, he is now a director of the Hiroshima Peace
Culture Foundation.

Left: Kosaku Okabe, superintendent of education in the town of Miwa, Kyoto Prefecture, addresses schoolchildren. Right: Sakae Hosaka lives in Tokyo with her husband, a director of the Tokyo Council of A-Bomb Sufferers Associations.

Left: Teiichi Teramura, standing in front of his home in Kyoto, works part time in a post-retirement job. Right: Nakaichi Nakamura, who also holds down a postretirement job, plays with his grandchildren in front of his Tokyo home.

Clockwise from left: Masae Kawai lives in the city of Mitaka, Tokyo; her mother, also a survivor, is visiting her. Fumiko Nonaka, an officer of the Osaka Association of Atomic Bomb Sufferers, attends an antinuclear rally. Asae Miyakoshi lives in Tokyo with her husband; she is in and out of hospital. Sumiko Umehara is an officer of the Kanagawa Prefectural Association of Atomic Bomb Sufferers. Misue Sagami is photographed at the nursing home in Tokyo where she was living at the time of her death in October 1984. Kayoko Satomi, a director of the Ichikawa Association of Atomic Bomb Sufferers, lives in Ichikawa, Chiba Prefecture, with her husband and children.

Clockwise from left: Machiyo Kurokawa, a director of the Kanagawa Prefectural Association of Atomic Bomb Sufferers, addresses an antinuclear group. Katsuyoshi Yoshimura teaches classical Japanese literature at a high school in Kyoto. Hiroshi Shibayama, a director of the Kyoto Prefectural Association of Atomic Bomb Sufferers, runs his own company in Kyoto. Kiyoko Sato, mother of three children, lives in Tokyo with her husband. Katsuo Fukushima, now completely blind, sits with his wife—also a survivor—on the verandah of their Tokyo home.

Akira Nagasaka, a middle school teacher in Tokyo, is a director of the Tokyo Council of A-Bomb Sufferers Associations. He is passing out leaflets calling for the enactment of a Hibakusha Aid Law and the abolition of nuclear weapons.

blanket apiece and had to huddle together for warmth. We worked mainly on construction sites, building roads and air-raid shelters, and were supervised by a Japanese civilian employed by the army. This man wore a uniform and carried a wooden sword. Occasionally someone from the military would also come to oversee us.

We were fed three times a day, at first on a mixture that was one-third rice and two-thirds wheat and kaoliang, and later on a thin gruel. The amount was too small to prevent us from rapidly becoming exhausted. Usually we were not released from work until one or two in the morning and hardly had time to doze off before being roused to start again at five. We gobbled our food standing up, and if we were late we were beaten with the wooden sword.

Once when we were digging a tunnel it collapsed. One of the workers, a man of about thirty, was pinned under the rockfall, unconscious. The Japanese overseer merely commented that he wasn't going to die and yelled at us to get back to work. He would not let us take the man to the hospital. When we tried to insist, he screamed at us for insubordination and insulted our nationality. Seething, we held ourselves in check and took up our tools again. Sometimes the army or the military police would call one of us to the guardroom for punishment, and some returned beaten black and blue.

One unforgettable incident concerned Kim, a young man of about twenty-six. One evening I heard Kim talking in his sleep. Listening more intently, I realized he was calling out the names of his parents and wife back home.

"Hey, Kim, what's wrong?" I woke him up and heard his story with growing anger. "I've always worked hard," he told me, "to help my parents. They're very old now. I was working in the fields three days after my wedding when a truck suddenly drew up beside me, and I was told brusquely that I was to be part of our district's requisition for military service. I never had a chance to return home and say goodbye to my wife and parents before being brought to Japan."

How could such things be permitted to happen? Besides

forced labor, there was also forced recruitment into the army. Even at the Kawanami Shipyard there was a subcontractor in charge of requisitioning Koreans to be used in either military or civilian work. Kim eventually went insane, and apparently there were many others like him.

Often in the barracks at night the older men would whisper among themselves that Japan could not win the war. All that sustained me was the thought that the tide of war was turning against Japan and defeat was imminent. It was becoming more and more difficult for me to work because I was so weakened, and I tried to think of ways of avoiding work.

On August 9 I went with Han, a compatriot from the same barracks, to the guard post at the wharf and persuaded the guard that we had to go into Nagasaki to see a friend. There was an air-raid warning that morning as we were making our way to the station, and we took shelter nearby. Then the all-clear sounded. As we were waiting for a streetcar, we heard a strange buzzing. I looked up into the sky and saw two or three streams of white smoke. First checking that no one could overhear, I commented in Korean, "It's an enemy plane!" Han replied in the same language, "There's something strange about the sound. I think we should take cover." We set off running in the direction of the Oura district but had gone no more than four or five meters when we saw a brilliant flash like lightning. This is the end, I thought, and found myself lying face down on the streetcar tracks. I have no clear memory of what happened for the next ten minutes. Han's voice calling my name brought me to my senses, and I sat up. I took a quick look around and saw that the city was covered by a dark red pall of smoke and dust.

"Come on, try to move. We can't stay here." Han was pulling at me urgently. I stood up, tottering, and with Han's shoulder as support joined the frantic flight of people to the cemetery on a small hill nearby. I could not help noting the fallen bodies of the injured and the stain of blood everywhere. The enormous pine trees in the cemetery had snapped at the roots and fallen over, and the tombstones were overturned. There must have been twenty or thirty people there, all of whom seemed to have escaped with nothing but the clothes on their backs. The hideous wounds and burns that disfigured them defy description. It was then that the pain, which had been dormant until then, attacked me savagely. Unable to endure its fury, I moaned, *"Aigo, aigo"*—it hurts—in my own language. At that, for some reason, the Japanese people beside us hastily moved away. In confusion, we took a look at ourselves. My face and the left half of my body were swollen and dark red from burns, and my left arm was badly blistered. I was a frightening sight.

We remained in that graveyard for several hours, until finally I collapsed again. Han tried to bring me around, telling me that I could not die there. "We're the only Koreans here," he said. "There's no one to help us but ourselves." At about seven in the evening we were told that the injured should go to an aid station that had been set up at the Katsuyama Primary School. Staggering, we set off. The seriously injured were being carried on stretchers, but when we asked for one, we were told that we were young and could walk. And so, gritting our teeth, we walked.

On reaching the school, we went immediately to the air-raid shelter under the building. In the darkness were crowded sixty or seventy people, whimpering and crying. Moans of pain, cries for parents, pleas for help rose from all sides. There was virtually no sleep to be had that night. The next morning, when we went into the schoolyard, we saw the dead bodies of several people near a sink. They must have died after relieving their thirst there.

Han, who was not as badly injured as I, went back to Koyagi to tell our friends what had happened. In the meantime a truck came to take the injured to the primary school in Isahaya, north of Nagasaki, where we found the bare floors of the classrooms packed with forty or fifty people lying crowded together. Every room was the same. I recorded my name and address at the reception area at the entrance and then for the first time received medical attention. This, as I heard later, was no more than a swab of charred tea leaves mixed with oil and applied to open wounds. I also ate my first meal. Members of the women's auxiliary had prepared rice balls but became nauseated when they tried to approach the injured. It was hardly possible to call what lay there human.

That night I spent in darkness again, surrounded by cries and moans. My own pain was hard enough to bear, but it was my thoughts that tortured me the most. What purpose did all this suffering serve? I finally slept, and when I woke it was morning. I found myself tightly embracing the person lying next to me. He was already a cold corpse.

I crawled to the toilet. While there I heard from the next room moans of *"Aigo, aigo."* Koreans! With beating heart I went into the room. There I saw forty or fifty men lying completely naked. They were laid out like lumps of burned flesh. My voice penetrated the whimpering, and I was surrounded by tearful pleas for help.

The men told me they had been brought to Japan for forced labor and could not speak a word of Japanese. When the bomb fell, they had been doing construction work outside the Mitsubishi Armaments factory. Working in the hot sun, they had been wearing little more than trousers and as a result had suffered hideous burns all over. After they had been brought to the school and shut away in that room, no one came near them, and they were unable to ask for help. Despite their nakedness and injuries, they were still human beings, and I became angrier and angrier. There also welled up within me a feeling of tenderness for these my compatriots.

Someone was crying out for water, but I persuaded him that it was dangerous to drink. Instead I had some tea made and allowed him just to wet his lips. Then I went to the reception area to negotiate with the Japanese official there.

"Have you taken the names and addresses of those people?" I asked.

"No. To begin with, we can't make ourselves understood. Besides, we're afraid."

Suppressing my anger, I continued. "What do you intend to do? You are the ones who brought these people to Japan against their will. Do you really think you can let it go at that? Why have you made us suffer in this way? These people don't have long to live. It's not likely they'll ever have another life. Are you just going to let them die?''

"There's nothing we can do."

I felt my heart break. "You can't just do nothing! It's unforgivable. It's discrimination against Koreans."

"Well, what do you suggest we do?" He was bristling with anger and moved closer to me.

"You're a local-government official, aren't you? There has to be a Korean organization somewhere around here, surely. Contact the person in charge and get an interpreter. At least do your duty and get their names and addresses."

At last the official agreed and got up to do something.

Although they searched high and low for an interpreter, they could find no one, so it was finally I who went around collecting the information and laboriously writing it down. The day was scorching, and my burns were swelling. Overnight, maggots had begun to breed in them. I had taken down the particulars of no more than twelve people when I collapsed, unconscious. I do not know what happened to my Korean brothers after that, but I imagine they all died. I developed a high fever and was unable to move. The next day, August 12, I think, I was taken to the navy hospital in Isahaya. Here they did no more than bathe my wounds. I certainly was given no treatment worthy of the name.

During the afternoon of August 15, one of the nurses came in crying. "You people will be happy," she exclaimed. "We have lost the war. You will be free to go home. I don't know how we are going to bear it!" A sudden exhilaration shimmered through me. "You mean it?" Bewildered but happy, I sought confirmation of the good news again and again. I remembered the whispered talk of the older men in the barracks at Koyagi. "It'll be over soon. Japan will lose." Then it had seemed like a dream; I had never thought it would become reality so quickly. I remembered the inhumanity suffered by my compatriots, their countless days of suffering, capped finally by the cruel hell of the atomic bomb.

I told myself that for every Korean killed, hundreds of Japanese must have died—old people, women, and children, all noncombatants, all slaughtered. The massacred knew no national boundaries. Nor was there any difference in the pain and sadness of those who lost people close to them or who suffered injury. Who bears the burden of responsibility for the indiscriminate slaughter of the pawns of Japanese imperialism? America, are you satisfied now?

Overwhelmed by my thoughts, I could not keep still. I was compelled by a dazzling inner voice repeating, ''Korean liberation.'' I left the hospital the next day. ''For years I've lived like a slave, and I've survived. Now at last we can start to build a new nation. I have to get well quickly so I can be of use.'' Inspired by my decision, I made my way back to Nagasaki. All day I walked among the burned-out ruins as I scoured the city seeking news of my friends. On August 17 I crossed to Koyagi.

Almost everyone I talked to in the Korean laborers' barracks was filled with enthusiasm to go home, overjoyed at the coming of liberation. Friends urged me to go back with them, but I had a wife and children, at present evacuated to the countryside, to consider, and my wounds were severe. I decided to wait a little to see how things turned out. I returned to Nagasaki and sought out a friend with whom I stayed about ten days, recuperating. Then I took on such manual labor as my condition permitted.

In September or October I was hit badly by symptoms of radiation sickness. Since then I have been hospitalized many times. Recently I have begun suffering from absent-mindedness and high blood pressure. My hands rapidly become numb, and I often drop things as a result. I can hardly use my legs. The left half of my body, which was burned, has become paralyzed, and the scars are discolored. In winter my body chills like a corpse. Some twenty or thirty Koreans of my acquaintance who live in Japan are also atomic bomb victims, and since they belong to the national health scheme and have been officially designated as sufferers of atomic bomb disease, they can receive free treatment. However, beyond that they get absolutely nothing.

On this score, there is very little security guaranteed by either the central government or local governments, and whether the Japanese government is willing to take responsibility for those Koreans who were used in forced labor during the war is a major issue. The Koreans who returned home are in an even more tragic predicament. There are some twenty thousand atomic bomb victims in Korea who receive absolutely no relief, yet they are suffering from radiation-induced disorders as well as difficulties in everyday life. The atomic bomb question does not lie in the past. Its victims are still alive and will demand our attention in the future as well. I ask everyone's warm support to help them.

Lee Gi-sang died of stomach cancer in December 1982. He was sixty-seven years old.

Forty Years of Grief

Sumiko Umehara

I was nineteen when I married a soldier. Two weeks after our son's birth the following year, my husband embarked for the front, and I remained in rented rooms in the district of Koi in Hiroshima, awaiting his return. He was never to come back to us, for he was killed at Leyte Gulf.

Eight fifteen on the morning of August 6, 1945. I will never forget that moment. I was hanging out the baby's diapers on the balcony when I noticed what seemed to be a multicolored parachute floating in the sky to the east above Gokoku Shrine. I laughingly remarked to the woman watering her plants on the balcony of the house next door that the kind Americans might be dropping chocolates, thinking we didn't have much in the way of such things. My ten-month-old son, inside the house, began to cry as if burned. I had just turned to see to him when a sudden shock from behind propelled me into the room. Tottering, I threw myself down on the baby.

It was a little while before I looked down at him. I was amazed to see blood streaming from his forehead. I also realized that various parts of my own body hurt. I thought that a bomb must have exploded. As I gathered up the baby and searched for the first-aid kit, the air of the room became heavy with purple smoke. My first thought was poison gas. Afraid of being trapped inside, I took the baby downstairs and out into the street. Then the house collapsed and began to burn.

By the stone wall opposite I noticed the dead body of a man of about fifty, still sitting cross-legged with his arms folded around himself. I also saw a young woman, perhaps in her late teens, who seemed to be in great pain, with strips of skin hanging down from her chest like old rags. She gripped me and called out for water. I did not know what to do, so I broke away and fled to the nearest hilly area.

In the comparative safety of the hillside, I found that the injured who had already arrived there were dying in agony. What I saw around me was a scene of living hell. Though I had no idea what would become of us, I felt relieved at my narrow escape. It was about then that my baby started having diarrhea. Without even a roof over my head, there was little I could do, especially as there was no possibility of treatment. I washed his soiled diaper in a small stream nearby and dried it by attaching a line to the branches of a tree.

The next day, worry about my father prompted me to set off with my baby for his house in Kusunoki-cho. On the way there I came across a cousin, the first relative I had met since the explosion, and was told that my father had died. When the implications of his death hit me, I decided that there was no place in the world for my son or myself; I had been intending to ask my father for help. The only way out seemed to be to die with my baby. I made my way to my mother's grave at Mitaki but found it impossible to carry out my plan when I looked down at my son's face. Whatever the future held, I could not take his life. I plodded back to Koi.

Since Hiroshima had been completely destroyed, there was no work to be had. There seemed to be no point in staying there, where I could do nothing, so I decided to go to neighboring Okayama Prefecture, where I had relatives. Some of them agreed to look after my baby, though it broke my heart to leave him. Nevertheless, I was sure that things could only get better. That was about forty years ago, but I can still see the puckered, crying face of my son as I placed him in my aunt's arms. It was the last time we were to meet in this world. He died two years later.

Why had my child been born? Was it to save me from what would have been instant death if I had still been outside when the bomb fell? If there had been no war, he would have been able to grow up in happiness. Life had been cruel to him. I found out later that he had lived and died in poverty. Many were the nights I wept for him, cradling the urn containing his tiny bones. I promised him that we would be together in the next world, my son who could not be with me or find joy in this one.

Later I went to live with my brother in Tokyo. There I met my present husband. When I married him, I vowed that this time I was going to find happiness. However, though he seemed good and kind, he gave himself up to drinking, gambling, and other women, so that my hardships continued without relief. I thought much of his trouble stemmed from our not being able to have children. In the third year of our marriage we adopted one of his nieces. She came to me when she was a week old, and I brought her up as if she were my own. I was bolstered by the joy of thinking that my husband would now be content.

About that time, my father-in-law was foisted on us. He had not got along with the wife of my husband's older brother, with whom he had been living, and came to us after lengthy dispute. I could not refuse to house the old man, but it fell on my shoulders to look after him. My life gradually became harder and harder to bear. Even so, I strove to make my father-in-law as happy as possible. Eventually he began to act violently. He would threaten us with a knife, kick over the dining table with all the food I had painstakingly prepared, and try to throw the kettle full of boiling water at us. This behavior continued daily for five fearful years. On the days when he was not physically violent he would grumble from early morning, finally driving my husband out of the house and leaving me to cope with him as best I could.

As my father-in-law continued to deteriorate, our daily life became more and more difficult, until we finally had to move to a house little better than a hovel. When his violence grew unbearable, I talked with my brother-in-law and had my father-in-law taken to a mental hospital, where he was diagnosed as schizophrenic. He was too ill to live a normal family life and had to be institutionalized. The hospital was expensive, but I decided that he had to have treatment. Even though I myself was in pain, I pared our family expenses to a minimum. All the time he was in hospital, I took food to him, delicacies like fruit and rice balls wrapped in seaweed, which we could not even afford for ourselves.

When finally he approached death, he was transferred to my brother-in-law's house. When I visited him two or three days before he died, he twice thanked me for looking after him for so long. I began to cry, overwhelmed by these unexpectedly kind words from a father-in-law who had always seemed unfeeling.

Five years later, I began to suffer from prolonged constipation. After a large bowel movement of what looked like jet black sand, I went to the hospital, where I was shocked to learn that my symptoms were radiation induced. One day I passed a clot of blood as large as a baby's head. I continued to hemorrhage for the next two years. Then suddenly one winter morning as I was using the toilet I heard a sound like the tinkling of fragments of glass. The bleeding stopped completely. My weakened body regained its strength as the days passed, and ten years after I had been diagnosed as suffering radiation sickness I was given a clean bill of health. Though I had been near death, the two years of hemorrhaging had probably cleansed my blood.

I continue to enjoy good health, and my daughter is now married, with three children of her own. At last, surrounded by my grandchildren, I am leading a truly happy life. However happy I may be, though, I cannot stop grieving for my little son.

I am now working for the welfare of atomic bomb survivors as an official of a victims' support group. A few years ago I had the responsibility of visiting the homes of all the survivors in the area, and found many suffering from poor health and disrupted family life. When I met an old woman who had been left to fend for herself, having lost her entire family to the bomb, I realized how fortunate I was by comparison.

I hope to spend the rest of my life giving encouragement to survivors who are beset by problems and urging the government to render aid so that we can all live in peace and happiness. I pray that war will never again occur, and that no one will ever again die as meaninglessly as those who were killed by the atomic bomb.

A Voice from the Flames

Shige Hiratsuka

We were a family of four, that morning of August 6, 1945. It was a little past eight o'clock. Breakfast was just over, and my husband was glancing through the newspaper while I cleared up after the meal. Our two children were playing nearby.

Just then a brilliant flash like lightning appeared and the thunderous roar of an explosion reverberated around us. In a moment our house collapsed, and we found ourselves buried in its rubble. As my husband and I worked frantically to free ourselves, I heard a cry for help from the woman next door. I called back to her, "If we get out before you, we'll come and help you." When we did finally pull ourselves free, we saw the city of Hiroshima in ruins around us. Nowhere was a building left intact, and in several places tongues of fire had begun to lick outward. Suddenly panic-stricken, and completely forgetting about our neighbor, I began searching for my children.

As I was calling their names, a voice emerged from a spot two or three meters away. "Help, Mummy, help." It was my six-year-old daughter Kazuko. Hurrying to the spot, I found her tightly wedged from the chest down by fallen plaster and timber. I screamed to my husband to come quickly and do something. He, however, could hardly move, being badly bruised and

141

bleeding from the shoulder. He had no strength left; it was all he could do to walk.

My daughter kept calling to me. "It hurts, Mummy. My legs hurt. I can't move. Hurry and get me out." I tugged at her but could not move her. No matter how desperately I tried, I just could not free her. The fires were moving closer and closer. We would not be able to stay there much longer. Finally, when the flames began to lap around us, we were stirred into moving, no longer able to stand the intense heat. I realized I was afraid to die. I could not let myself be burned alive.

Tears streaming from my eyes, I placed my hands together as if in prayer and asked my daughter to forgive me. "Kazu, I am a bad mother to you, but please forgive me. You don't want to die either, I know. Mummy isn't brave enough to stay here and die with you. I'm afraid of the fire. Kazu, forgive me, forgive me." Then I chose an area that seemed to be safe from fire and fled toward it, pulling my husband along by the hand. I kept looking back at the ruins of our house as if I were being dragged by the hair from behind. There had been no time to rescue our other child, either.

In my flight I stepped on or stumbled over corpses countless times without knowing what they were. Even when I realized I was lying on a mutilated body, I could feel no revulsion, only pity.

Eventually we reached the river bank. My throat raw and my mouth parched, I bent down to take some water from the stream. Bodies were floating past on the current, so many that I had to push them aside with my hands to find space enough to take water into my cupped hands. But no sooner had I pushed aside one corpse than another took its place. All were badly burned and swollen. When I finished drinking, I remained staring vacantly at the bodies. Then I suddenly became sick to my stomach and began to vomit a yellow, bubbly liquid. I had no reserves of energy or spirit left. I did not even want to cry. The sound of someone screaming finally made me look up. A woman, almost delirious, was searching the corpses one by one for members of her family.

Most of the corpses were covered with hideous burns, and the intestines of some were spilling out. Had those people also rushed desperately to this spot and, reaching the end of their strength, collapsed and died here? Sitting there alive, with my children dead in the fire, I cursed the war and what it could do to people. All I wanted was to be somewhere where war was not.

The sky darkened and a heavy black rain began to fall, pounding the earth. It did not last long. We spent the night there on the river bank, a long night during which we did not sleep. I cried loudly most of the time, uttering a stream of apologies to my dead children. "I'm sorry, Kazu. Forgive Mummy. I was cruel to leave you. It tortured me. You must have suffered so." My husband said absolutely nothing, but tears streamed down his cheeks.

Sleepless and bitten by insects, we endured the long night. At about nine o'clock the next morning a group of relief workers came. They loaded the survivors onto a truck and took us to a small village some kilometers from Hiroshima. We were housed in a school gymnasium. The scene was hellish: there were people with ghastly wounds, burned people, people already dead. In the midsummer heat, maggots were breeding in the burned flesh of the dead. From every direction rose the moans of the injured asking for relief, begging for water. A child, not knowing its mother had died, crawled up to her and lay limply against her to suck from a breast that must have been dry. I could not cry. I could only wonder abstractedly how much longer such a war could continue. While I was lost in my thoughts, people continued to die.

We spent several days there, enveloped by heat and an indescribable stench. Eventually those who had relatives they could go to or a home to return to were told to leave, since the trains were now running again. We decided to go to my husband's hometown of Sanuma in Miyagi Prefecture, in northern Japan.

There we became a little more rested and calm. I decided to wash my filthy hair, but when I put a comb through it, it came out in clumps. In surprise, I pulled at my hair and more came out. It was all too much, and I broke down in tears. Very soon I had gone bald. A little while after that, we were admitted to the university hospital in Sendai. The hospital staff did not know what to make of our injuries or how to deal with them, and for the first week only our wounds were treated. To determine what was wrong, we were advised to have blood tests. My husband and I lay down side by side, and my husband had his blood taken first. When the needle was withdrawn after the sample had been taken, the bleeding would not stop. Nothing, including direct pressure on the spot, was of any use. No one knew what to do. While doctors continued to come and go, my husband's body began to erupt all over in purple spots. He then vomited a lot of brown liquid, went limp, and died an hour later. Even my husband had been taken from me by the bomb.

I was six months pregnant at the time. At a time when there was a severe food shortage, I worried whether the meager amount I was eating was enough to give my baby the nourishment it needed. My baby boy, born in December, was below average in birth weight, and I was slow to recover from his birth. I remained in the hospital several months. My baby beside me, I cried uncontrollably much of the time, alone and afraid of the future. What could I do in my condition? I had no family of my own to turn to.

In April my in-laws urged me to recuperate in their home, and I left the hospital. But living conditions in their house became more and more difficult. My husband's oldest brother was repatriated from Manchuria in August with his wife and three children, followed soon by another brother-in-law with his wife and four children. It was not easy for me there, sharing what little food there was. It was with bitterness that I continued to make my home there with my baby. Putting together meals in the kitchen, I wept to remember our life in Hiroshima. I had forgotten how to laugh.

My health is poor even today. I suffer from leukopenia, a low white cell count condition—a disease the war bequeathed me. I am convinced that those who were killed in the war and by the atomic bombs were nothing but pitiful pawns. I want to con-

tinue living as a memorial to my dead husband and children,
striving with all my might to ensure that war never again occurs.
If the suffering of the victims of the bomb were forgotten, it
would be so easy for war to break out. I pray that survivors will
speak out about their suffering to help build a world that will
never again know war.

A Message to the Young

Sachiko Masaki

Not long ago I had a letter from a friend I had been at school with in Nagasaki. Enclosed with the letter was a photo of a doll. The doll had a childlike innocence, its eyes closed, its hands clasped together, its knees bent in prayer. It had been made as a prayer for peace.

Like me, my friend had been through the hell of the atomic bombing of Nagasaki. She had lost her parents, brothers, and sisters, as well as many teachers, friends, and neighbors. She had been traumatized in body and mind but had managed to pull herself back up from the depths. The doll embodied her plea for peace. "Let the new generation find happiness. What happened must never be repeated," she wrote.

I always find myself in a quandary when I try to talk about my experiences as a victim of the atomic bomb. I want to tell what it was like, but I cannot find the words. How can I possibly make others understand? I tend to give up halfway. Yet now, after so many years have passed, I feel an urgent need to pass on to others what happened. I want to stand before each and every person on the face of the earth and tell of the madness and horror of war. "Yours bitterly," I salute all, as I speak for the three hundred thousand and more people who lost their lives when atomic bombs were dropped on August 6 and 9, 1945.

That year I was fourteen. As July drew to a close, the air raids on Nagasaki became more and more intense. One of the students mobilized to do war work, I was working in the precision machinery section of the torpedo factory at the Mitsubishi Armaments branch factory located a kilometer and a half from the hypocenter. Though not old enough to understand the meaning of death, I was nevertheless prepared to die as I devoted myself to my country. I felt that we were fighting a holy war to attain peace.

Because of the repeated air raids, the streetcars were not running, and I often made the two-hour journey to the factory from my home in the Narutaki district on foot. It was a considerable strain on my body, weakened already by malnutrition owing to the food shortage. Even friends who could hardly walk because of beriberi shuffled along. Many walked barefoot.

August 9 was a fine day. Air-raid sirens had been wailing since early morning, and we had been taking shelter in a ''tunnel factory'' fifteen minutes' walk from our workplace. When the all-clear sounded, we returned to the factory and settled down to our work with relief. It was when we were standing up to have our work inspected that I was hurled to the concrete floor. There was a roaring in my ears, and the windows glowed a luminous red. Crushed against the debris of the factory by the force of the explosion, I thought I was going to die.

I do not know how much time passed. Straining with all my might, I pulled myself up. Screams and groans reverberated around me. At first I did not know where I was, so great was the destruction. Fingers of fire had begun to reach out here and there. Preparing to make my way through the flames, I pulled on my protective hood. One of the supervisors, drenched in blood, was calling out, ''Try to get to the tunnel factory.'' I ran there frantically. The tunnel was dark and quiet. In the gloom I made out the agitated figure of a middle-aged woman holding a child and crooning to it over and over again the national anthem and a popular war song. Suddenly I began to worry about my mother.

I met a classmate in the tunnel. Together we set out for home. Spread out under the sparkling midsummer sun was a scene of such horror that it was beyond my ability to take it in. I still recall it as if a scroll of scenes of hell were being unrolled before me. The bodies of people and horses were strewn everywhere. All the people were naked, and they were covered with burns and wounds. Their faces were burned dark brown and swollen like balloons. The living were wandering around like ghosts, burns all over them and their skin hanging in tatters. A relief train moved slowly along, carrying injured people. When I met others, I would inquire about the damage to my part of the city and ask for water. Quenching my thirst, I was able to continue. I noticed, though, that whenever I drank, for some reason I began to vomit.

I had heard that the damage was too severe for me to hope to make my way along the main road where the streetcar lines were, so I approached my home over hillside tracks. On the way I met several friends, all injured. I found my way to our school and asked the principal to send them help. He in turn asked me to notify the parents of one of my friends of their child's death. I went to her house. I cannot forget her father, motionlessly looking out at the destruction, saying resignedly, "So there's no hope, then." I had walked to the factory every morning with this friend.

It was about seven o'clock in the evening when I reached home. My mother was sitting on the stone steps in front of the entrance, waiting for me. She pulled herself up. Her face, alight with joy at my safety, still remains in my heart. I realized then that I was smeared with blood and oil from the factory. However, I had miraculously escaped severe external injuries and was only bruised. Strangely, the cuffs of my baggy trousers were filled with tiny slivers of glass.

The tiles of our roof had been wrenched away by the explosion and lay around like fish scales. Pillars were broken, and the inside of the house was covered with so much broken glass that it was impossible to walk around in bare feet. So I went inside still wearing my wooden clogs. Since we could not get rid of the pieces of glass no matter how hard we cleaned, for several days we continued to wear footgear inside, contrary to custom. Our wall clock remained lying where it had fallen on the tatami-matted floor, registering the hour and minute of the explosion.

When it rained, we had nothing to shield us, for our house was no longer a shelter. For the last week of the war we slept, together with our neighbors, in the air-raid shelter dug into the hillside behind our house. The shelter was dark and had a stale smell. The roughness of the ground hurt our bodies, and we were forced to curl up because of the cramped space. I had no appetite and vomited up the water that I drank. About three weeks later I began to lose color and feel dizzy. It became increasingly difficult to breathe. I had no strength and could not even get out of bed.

Those who experienced the atomic bomb suffered a decrease in their white cell count. Their hair fell out. Nosebleeds would not stop, and wounds would not heal. There was subcutaneous hemorrhaging. Burns healed into keloids. Day after day, people died around me. The school became a hospital. In the school-yard were hand-drawn rubbish carts. The bodies of those who died were taken out on stretchers and piled onto the carts. I remember their rigid feet sticking out. I heard that members of the local women's group were working among the injured in the auditorium and the classrooms, extracting the maggots that had begun to breed in the wounds.

My older brother, who was at the naval academy on Etajima island, about ten kilometers south of Hiroshima, returned home with a group of his friends whose homes were in the devastated area. The friends searched frantically for their families. I heard that the family of one of them had been completely wiped out and that all he found was his mother's arm. He knew it was his mother's by the wristwatch on it. My cousin and others were working at the Saiwai-machi factory of Mitsubishi Shipbuilding, about a kilometer and a half from the hypocenter, when the bomb fell. Several years passed before my cousin told me what had happened. They had tried to help a man trapped under the rubble of a building. All their efforts were useless. The fires grew more threatening. In desperation the man, whose legs were trapped, begged them to cut off his legs with a saw. One of them did as he asked. They thus succeeded in extricating him, but he bled to death.

I regained my health toward the end of the year, thanks to my mother's devoted care and to the food that relatives in the country sent us.

Some time ago, browsing in a bookstore, I found a book about Japan's postwar constitution. Reading Article 9, the one renouncing war and the use of force as a means of settling international disputes, I unexpectedly found tears in my eyes. When I returned home, I showed it to my daughter, then a student. She commented, "It would be wonderful if every country had a constitution like Japan's."

The present government is justifying rearmament as necessary for the protection of the country and the maintenance of peace. I heard the same words at the time of World War II. They call those arms "defensive," arms that in reality are murderous weapons intended for slaughter. An individual who stored weapons in the same way would be called a criminal. Why should a country be allowed to engage freely in this activity? I want to open the eyes of those who go along with the current trend in public affairs. Why is it that people find it difficult to persevere in their demands for peace? I am worried that the dark flow of events leading up to World War II will be repeated.

No one can remain an onlooker. Humankind should not be its own enemy. Problems that need joint resolution are piling up. We should act as human beings, not as national entities, linking hands to solve problems so that the happiness of all may be assured. How can we possibly think that a balance of arms can possibly guarantee peace? Armaments are being relentlessly built up both East and West in the name of maintaining a balance, and are threatening to overwhelm the globe. How ridiculous can you get? The results of an accidental release of nuclear terror are too horrible to imagine.

We are too concerned with our individual good and our national good. It has been said that the life of a single human being is worth more than the earth itself. War, though, reduces the value of life to zero. Each and every person was born and reared the child of his or her mother's love and hope. We should ponder the value of life. We should persevere in talking together to establish friendly relations so that there will be no need for armaments. International disputes should be settled through patient discussion at the United Nations, not through the barbarity of military power. History proves that armament leads to further armament and that revenge breeds revenge. The special terror of nuclear weapons is that even after the fighting is over, their effects continue through radiation-induced disorders and second-generation symptoms. It has been reported that the incidence of cancer among atomic bomb survivors is above average. I myself recently had an operation for cancer.

We have only one earth; for the sake of the future as well as the present, do not let it be contaminated.

I have heard that the official reason for excluding the atomic bomb question from Japanese textbooks is that it is too cruel an issue to expose children to. We should confront the truth. If we truly know our history, we ourselves can decide the path we will take. When I see teenagers, I think they are truly beautiful, with their plump cheeks and their smooth hair. My friends, those student-workers who were killed, crushed by the force of the blast or burned by the rays, were also beautiful. I place my hope in the younger generation and its ability to judge with clarity.

In conclusion, I would like to include a short essay I found in a collection of photos of the Nagasaki bombing. It was written by Michiko Ogino, ten years old at the time.

"My sister was buried under our house and was crying hysterically. The beam pinning her down would not budge. A sailor said, 'It's hopeless,' and went away. In the distance I saw someone running. It was a woman. She appeared to be naked. Her body was purple. 'Mother!' Now everything would be all right. The man from next door tried hard, but the beam would not move. He looked sorry. 'Give up. It's useless,' he said, and went off. The fires began to flare up. My mother grew pale. She looked down at my sister. My sister's small eyes looked up at her. My mother glanced across at the beam. She pushed against one spot with her right shoulder. She put all her strength into it. Moving slightly, the beam creaked, and my sister's leg was free. Exhausted, my mother sank down where she was. She had been picking eggplant for lunch in the fields when the bomb fell. Her hair had been frizzled red and short. The skin on her right shoulder, which had pushed the beam, had peeled off. You could see the flesh beneath. Red blood flowed and flowed. Her pain grew worse. She writhed in agony. That night she died.''

A Second-Generation Victim

Fumiko Harada

When she was hospitalized for the third time, on August 15, 1967, Junko promised us jauntily, "I won't be coming home till I'm completely well. If I'm not out in time for the festival, I'll get leave to go to it." Two months later she returned home on the eve of the festival as she had said she would—but as a corpse.

Junko's mother and I are sisters, both survivors of the atomic bombing of Hiroshima. For three days after the bomb was dropped, we roamed the devastated city with our younger sister, searching for our father and brother and my brother-in-law. I was nineteen at the time, my sister twenty-one.

Junko never had a day's illness from the time she was born. She drank her mother's milk lustily, becoming so plump and round that we used to tease her for being like the reigning sumo star of the time, Terukuni. She was the center of the whole family's affection. Suddenly in the autumn of 1965, the year before she was due to finish high school, she fell ill with hemolytic anemia and was given only three days to live. Her parents could not have been more astounded. When she was admitted to the Atomic Bomb Hospital, we could not even weep, so great was our shock.

All the anxiety that had been suppressed till then rose to the surface. Both her father and her mother wondered fearfully whether the illness had any connection with the atomic bomb. The physician in charge of Junko's case rejected that possibility. "There are about seventy people around the country with the same mysterious disease. This is the first time we've had a patient with those symptoms here." But his words did nothing to alleviate my fears.

It was around that time that the story of a leukemia victim, Fumiki Nagoya, born in 1960, came to my ears. His mother had been sixteen when caught in the blast of the bomb 2.3 kilometers from the hypocenter. I tried hard to stop myself from facing the possibility that Junko could be likewise affected. Refusing to utter the ominous words "the atomic bomb and its aftereffects," we rallied to give Junko the best care possible. Perhaps the emotions of everyone penetrated, or perhaps Junko's youth and her spirit to live overcame the disease, for the symptoms abated after a two-month hospitalization. She entered her third and last year of high school, going to the hospital for regular checkups. She would often stop in to visit me on her way home from school or the hospital.

In July 1966 a group concerned with the interests of children still in the womb when the bomb fell or conceived thereafter was formed. I went to the first meeting and spoke about Junko's illness. The Yamashita-kai, a study group formed by mothers living in Hiroshima, compiled stories of in utero victims in a book entitled *Until We Can Laugh* as a plea for increased aid and cooperation. From August 1 to 6 that year, as the group's representative, I called on members of the peace delegations who had come to Hiroshima from all over the nation for the anniversary of the bombing, urging them to aid in utero and second-generation victims. On August 6, undaunted by the blazing heat, Junko helped me, and that may have triggered her second hospitalization.

Although Junko would have preferred to enter the Atomic Bomb Hospital again, her doctor was on long-term sick leave, and it was decided that she should go to the Hiroshima Medical

University Hospital. She was released after a short while and distributed the eight-hundred-odd paper cranes she had folded while there to her cousins, Kazue and Reiko. I could well understand that she wanted no more of her illness.

After she left the hospital, her hard work to enter university was rewarded, and the following April, when the new academic year began, she became a college freshman. Her parents and relatives had wondered whether it might not be better for her to give up study and concentrate on fighting her illness, and they consulted her doctor. He saw no need for her to alter her course. When I think about it now, I am burdened with the conviction that that decision made it all the easier for the illness to take hold. She was to die the same year.

Article 25 of Japan's constitution states that "all people shall have the right to maintain the minimum standards of wholesome and cultured living." I cannot forgive the cruel behavior of the United States, which caused the atomic destruction and which even now menaces the rights of such insignificant people as my family and me. I am forced to worry excessively about the health of my two children because I am a bomb victim. I am filled with sorrow and indignation over what has happened.

Two days before Junko died, I visited her in her rain-darkened hospital room, little knowing that it was to be the last time we would meet on earth. "I'm so hot," Junko commented. Her cheeks were flushed, and she was sweating. It was, if anything, chilly outside because of the rain, and I felt a twinge of anxiety, wondering whether her body temperature regulation had been affected. "Junko, I've brought you a pear." She bit into the crisp fruit with relish. When I saw her eating, I berated myself for being an anxious old fool.

Junko would talk about anything under the sun with me: the Vietnam War, which had been the topic of a class debate; the problem of the outcasts in Japan; literature; films. My memories of her are endless. There must have been many things she wanted to do. Her death while still in her teens was a cruelty to which her parents and I could never become inured.

Some days after Junko entered the hospital for the third time, she phoned her mother and asked her to come and spend the night with her because she felt lonely. After that, I decided to try to get to the hospital as often as I could. "Mother, Auntie Fumiko, you're there, aren't you?" Gazing up at the two faces ranged above her, Junko would look relieved.

Junko's ward was in the new wing of the hospital, a bright, sparkling room with central heating and cooling. Of the six patients in the ward, Junko was the youngest, and the others doted on her. She was still very cheerful, talking and laughing a lot, the picture of a young student, not a sick person. When she was admitted, the doctor asked, "Are you in middle school?" I remember how firmly she replied that she was a college freshman. During her first hospitalization she had been taught how to make ornaments out of colored paper. She was very good with her hands and was delighted to give her tiny paper umbrellas and tasseled drums to the nurses and the other patients. She brought joy to the melancholy atmosphere of the ward with her words and her consideration.

I was reading a book lent me by a friend when from beside me came her voice: "Auntie, read me some, too." I did as she asked, but before I had even finished the second page, she said, "I can't keep the story straight. I'll read it myself when I get better." Another time, when she had finished reading part of a book, she tried to sit up in bed to take her medicine, but it cost her such effort that everyone in the room felt her pain.

In the middle of September Junko began to urinate less, her appetite dwindled, and she weakened before our eyes. Her doctor recommended she have a private room, since she needed to have peritonital irrigation. "Some patients show a definite improvement after the operation," said the doctor, asking for our consent. "The urine starts flowing freely again and the kidneys improve. But in Junko's case, unfortunately, I don't think there's any hope of a miracle." I was beside her when the operation was carried out on September 28. They opened a hole in the wall of her stomach and inserted a tube. After irrigation, the accumulated urine was drained with the same tube.

At the beginning of the operation, Junko held my hand tightly and asked the doctor if everything was all right. As the operation progressed, she moaned in fear and pain, and sweat covered her forehead. But she held on, muting her cries with great determination.

On September 29, on a friend's recommendation, I went to a Shinto shrine in the mountains of northern Hiroshima Prefecture to pray for Junko's recovery. So remote was the shrine that there were only two buses a day. A service for divine protection was performed, and I was given sacred water. In my diary, the entry for that day reads, "Now God is all we can depend on. I will do whatever I can for Junko. So must my husband and our friends, so that none of us will be sorry we didn't do all we could. We can only hope for a miracle."

I returned home at eight o'clock in the evening and went immediately with my husband to the hospital to give the sacred water to Junko. She was sleeping quietly. We slipped silently out of the room to the dark, quiet corridor and sat down on a bench with Junko's parents. My brother-in-law dejectedly lit a cigarette. Her voice full of feeling, my sister murmured, "Junko doesn't have much time left now. Since we were told she had only three days to live when she was in the second year of high school I've been more or less resigned to losing her."

On September 30, a Saturday, I was met by a sight that chilled me when I entered Junko's room. Junko's father and brother were there. There was a plug in her nose, she was vomiting blood, towels and ice packs were being held to her face, and she was being given oxygen. I was shocked a second time that Junko could spare the words of greeting she gave me. I decided to spend as long as I could by her side.

"October 1. First bowel movement since the operation. Great happiness. All three of us gave thanks to God," I wrote in my diary. That day Junko, my sister, and I had joined voices in a prayer of thanks.

"October 2. Some improvement in Junko's condition. Both urination and bowel movement. Prayed to God that the improvement would continue."

Junko had been vomiting severely night and day. As soon as

food or medicine entered her mouth, she brought it up. She was receiving intravenous nutrients and medication. We did our best to encourage her. We ordered nourishing and easily digested food, but since she had no appetite, the sight of it only saddened her, and her health continued to fail.

"Junko, have some cake, then," urged her mother. Junko reacted as if her feelings had been hurt and protested again and again that she did not want to be talked to like a baby. Instantly her mother corrected herself and offered the cake again in a normal voice. Often when we thought Junko was quietly sleeping, she would be gazing with wide eyes at the ceiling or the white walls. What was she thinking about? She had previously replied clearly to the questions of her doctor and the young woman physician who accompanied him, but as her illness worsened, her voice became less audible. After a while the young woman did not come any more.

Junko no longer wanted her friends to visit, nor did she want to see her relatives. It seemed to me that she had resigned herself to death. She had organized her diaries and photo albums after her second release from the hospital. Her state of mind was unfathomable.

"Auntie Fumiko, when I die, give all my things to Kazue" (my daughter). Twelve years separated the two girls. Four days before Junko died, she said to her father, "Daddy, I'm sorry." She then asked her mother to give her kimono to Kazue and her doll collection to her friends.

"Your daughter is very strong," said the hospital supervisor. "It is a very debilitating disease." Never complaining about her sickness, just lying quietly in bed, Junko gradually spoke less and less. To check that she was still conscious, we made a bell out of betel nuts and waved it in front of her, enticing a reaction. She replied quite clearly, "Those are the betel nuts Uncle Ryuzo brought back from Amami Oshima. Red ones. Blue ones. Yellow ones. Brown ones. Pale blue ones." Her words brought us relief; it was as if she were responding to our need.

Junko became sensitive about the color of her urine and what she vomited, and wanted to verify things for herself. "What symptoms do you get with uremic poisoning?'' She would fluster me with her questions. If we commented that she hiccuped a lot, she would tell us that it was because there was pressure on her diaphragm. When fluid began to accumulate in her abdomen, she knew all about it. I realized that she would accept no lies about her condition.

Her doctor recommended another peritonital irrigation, but my sister refused. ''If there were a chance of recovery, it would have some meaning. But as things are, it will just cause her more pain. She's too weak to take any more.'' Junko also adamantly refused.

On Saturday, I heard later, she greeted her brother, Koji, with a beautiful smiling face and spent what was to be her final day with her mother and brother, in cheerful spirits.

Her father told me she had given her brother the box of Morozoff chocolates that a friend of mine had brought her. With her usual parting words in my ears, ''Auntie Fumiko, come early tomorrow, won't you?'' I started crying as I went out into the darkened corridor. Poor Junko, there was nothing more we could do for her. She dominated my thoughts; several times I had forgotten to pay my streetcar fare or had forgotten to turn off the gas in the kitchen when leaving the house and had had to go back to do it. Ironically, on October 15 Junko's father, who usually did not visit her during the day because of his work as a grocer, went to take her the festive boxed lunch that his brother had made up for her. Thus he was there when she died.

I was not there at the end, though I had barely missed a day. She fell into her eternal sleep watched over by the parents who had surrounded her with their love. My sister said, ''We have to accept the inevitable. Junko has gone as a bride to a far, far place.''

I remember Junko and the conversations we had as clearly as if it were yesterday. The ballet shoes that she wore as a little girl are my tear-stained mementos. Junko fought her disease bravely, but by the end she was exhausted in body and spirit. She fought to the last despite the ravages of her illness. I wonder what sustained her.

Among the Flames

Tadaomi Furuishi

The morning sun on August 6, 1945, glinting in the deep blue of a cloudless sky, promised a day of fierce heat. I was seventeen at the time, a marine cadet in the Youth Administration Special Division attached to the Akatsuki Corps, based in the village of Tadanoumi, about fifty kilometers east of Hiroshima. That morning I was in the grounds of the local girls' secondary school, practicing signaling with fellow cadets.

A flash cut across the brilliant sunlight. None of us knew that it was the vile atomic bomb that exploded at that fateful moment, eight fifteen, devouring the lives of hundreds of thousands. Our training continued to the accompaniment of fifes; sweat streamed down our bodies.

At the end of the training session, we stood around waiting for the beginning of the next segment, antitank-attack practice. Most of our ships had been sunk or damaged, and all seaworthy vessels had been dispatched to the front. As a result, we had virtually nothing to use for our training and so were learning how to throw ourselves, armed with land mines, in front of the enemy tanks that were expected soon on the main islands.

Just then an order came from headquarters. We stopped in the middle of our exercises and were taken back into the school building. We learned that a new type of bomb had been dropped on Hiroshima and that we were to be sent there on the afternoon train as a relief team. One of those selected, I hurried back to the barracks, packed a knapsack with a change of clothes and some rice, and set off for the station in fine spirits.

It was already past two in the afternoon. The sun was blazing, and soon my tunic was dark with sweat. The train pulled into the station in a cloud of dirty smoke, crammed so full of people and luggage that it was hard to board. However, I had to get on somehow and hurriedly found an open window. I threw my bag in and clambered after it headfirst. The other occupants did not seem particularly upset by my unorthodox entry, perhaps because of my uniform or because I looked so boyish, but reached out and pulled me in by the arms. When I was able to catch my breath, I found to my dismay that my freshly laundered uniform was smeared with soot that no amount of rubbing could remove.

The train rumbled off. The carriage was packed, and I could not even squat down in the corridor. Sweat poured from me in the heat; I felt as if I were in a sauna.

Stopping often between stations, the train made its sluggish way along the coast. We members of the relief team were ordered off at a certain station. We lined up and proceeded into Hiroshima in file. We must have walked for about an hour, for when we reached the plaza in front of Hiroshima Station, the sun had almost set.

In the mountain of rubble that stretched all around, a square, blackened safe poked out its lonely head. Here and there tongues of red flame were lapping. The station buildings had been completely destroyed. Only one wall was still standing. The words on the signboards along the platforms had burned away, and a large locomotive lay on its side, bearing witness to the immense power of the bomb's blast.

Charred corpses were piled along the roadside and filled a collapsed air-raid shelter. When we stooped down to look more closely, the trouser-covered legs of the women shimmered an eerie white in the beams of our flashlights.

We met streams of people walking along. When I looked at

them, a shock ran through me. Their hair was burned and frizzled. The skin had peeled from their faces and was hanging in strips. Their mouths were contorted. White bones protruded from their faces. Their clothes were in shreds. Blood streamed from their heads. They held their arms out in front of them like ghosts, the skin hanging down. They wandered around dazed and uncertain, like sleepwalkers. It was like nothing on earth. My fear at the sight of these people sent a cold chill up my spine. I felt my body prickle with gooseflesh, and I gave an involuntary shiver.

We had been assigned to the company headquarters of the Hiroshima Relief Corps. We spent our first night in Hiroshima in tents on the East Drill Ground, near Hiroshima Station. When we awoke the next morning, it was already light. That day we were moved to an area next to a cemetery adjacent to the company headquarters and were sent into the city to search for materials with which to rebuild the headquarters. We had only seen the area around the station the night before and were shocked again as we walked through the city. Not a house was left standing. The pavement of the large bridges had been torn up and the stone balustrades twisted by the force of the blast.

According to one of the volunteer guards, it had been like experiencing an electric shock. There had been a flash and a noise like thunder, and then his house had collapsed around him, burying him under the debris. He had burrowed his way out.

Corpses that had yet to be taken away lay strewn along the roadside. There were some whose arms and legs had been torn off, some with their eyeballs bulging out, some as black as coal and shriveled to the size of a baby. Others, badly burned and desperately seeking water, had died as they thrust their faces into the water troughs kept for fire fighting. There was a black ball-shaped object on the stomach of one of the bodies; when we examined it, we found it was a mass of flies. Brushing the flies away, we saw underneath something that looked like an ice pack. It was the swollen intestines ripped from the abdomen, in which a multitude of maggots were seething.

We found the corpses of a mother and child beside the road.

The mother's face and body were covered with terrible burns; the child, hardly marked, had died enfolded in its mother's arms. That evidence of the depth of a mother's love brought tears to my eyes.

Water pipes had broken throughout the city, and the leakage had resulted in low water pressure. Water was not getting through to the places that really needed it, so we were divided into teams of two, given hammers and blocks of wood, and sent to scour the city seeking out leaks. Where pipes had broken and water was gushing out, we blocked the pipes with wood. Patrolling the city in this way, we saw many things. A burned-out streetcar was being dragged along by an amphibious tank; inside the streetcar we could see a heap of blackened bodies, some of which seemed still to be standing.

Many of the injured were being taken to schools, where the corridors and classrooms were so full that it was hard to find space to walk. Whimpers of pain and cries for water and help added to the hellish scene. The bodies of the recently dead lay quietly to one side. The blood that had seeped from their wounds meandered in thin streams along the floors of the rooms and corridors. The pervasive stench forced us to retreat to the schoolyard.

In a corner of the yard I noticed a small aluminum lunch box. It had probably been dropped by one of the injured. Inside I found rice and a piece of salmon that had turned to charcoal. It made such an impression on me that the memory remains vivid even today.

In the quiet of the ruined city we heard the sound of nails being hammered into wood. Thinking the hammering meant that reconstruction work was already under way, we looked to see what was happening and to our surprise saw someone making a coffin. With the majority of the incinerated dead nameless and disregarded, the person the coffin was being made for was perhaps truly lucky, I thought.

Walking along a back alley I heard moans from the vicinity of a demolished house. On investigating, I found an old woman in the debris, pinned from the waist down under the fallen building. She was near death. When she saw us, she cried out for water in a voice hardly louder than a mosquito's. We quickly squatted down beside her and held a water bottle to her mouth. She watched us with vacant eyes and soon stopped moving. She was dead. My comrade and I stood before her with hands joined in prayer. Those vacant eyes are seared into my memory.

Hiroshima is a city of many rivers. When we climbed up the banks to look down on the river flats, I could not contain a cry of horror. Countless people injured in the fires had flocked there seeking water. Cries for help, cries of pain, came from the wounded mass. Many did not move, perhaps already dead. Others lay in the water, easing the pain of their burned bodies. A baby crawled over its dead mother's stomach, searching for milk. In the river floated innumerable corpses, bobbing up and down on the current. It was truly hell itself.

Fiendish Yankees! I burned with loathing of the perpetrators of such a deed.

I did not know that I had been exposed to residual radiation. Day after day attacks of diarrhea continued. My bowel movements were like transparent gelatin, eventually with blood in them. Soon I found myself having to use the toilet dozens of times a day. The toilet at the headquarters was a temporary facility, a hole in the ground with two large planks thrown over it and straw mats hung around. There was always a long line of people suffering from diarrhea waiting to use it. I stood in line but often could not wait and rushed to a corner of the cemetery to relieve myself. By that time I could not swallow rice and was only able to eat small amounts of semiliquids, such as pumpkin soup and potato stew. As a result, my appearance grew cadaverous and I had difficulty carrying out my duties of moving food and medicines.

An unending stream of injured people poured into the headquarters. We helped the medical orderlies tend to them, though the treatment was no more than Mercurochrome and something the orderlies had put together. The liquid was poured into buckets, and we swabbed the injuries with a brush. Because many of the women had been wearing patterned work trousers, some had the pattern burned into their thighs like tattoos. Since it was summer, most people had been in short sleeves, and the exposed parts of their arms were burned, while the parts of their bodies covered by clothes, especially white clothes, were not seriously injured. After several days the burns festered and maggots bred in the wounds, and a stomach-turning stench pervaded the area.

Bodies were being brought from all around to the grounds near the headquarters, and we were employed digging trenches for them to be thrown into and burned. The bodies had already been out in the sun for several days when brought to us and were decomposed and covered with flies. Maggots were squirming in the eyes and nostrils; the smell was horrific. We carried the bodies on bamboo mats and wooden shutters to the trenches and ignited them with oil. The crackling of the burning bodies sounded like fish grilling.

Some of the bodies were those of students doing labor service. Before burning them we searched them for marks of identification, such as name tags on clothes or belongings. If we found something that could be used for identification, we placed it with the dead person's bones, which we put into rice bowls. Soon there were many women asking if we knew the fate of their children. We would take them to where we had placed the bones. It was painful to watch these women sink to the ground, tears streaming down their faces, as they clutched the charred air-raid hoods and other belongings of their dead children, crying out their names. When they had regained control, they came up to us and thanked us profusely before leaving. I remember how pleased we were at being able to help them in this way.

Soldiers below the rank of noncommissioned officer had to stand sentry every few nights. One night it was my turn to do the midnight watch. I felt uneasy because of the cemetery next to our tents. The night was very hot and humid. Soon after I went on duty it started drizzling, and as I felt the soundless drops hitting my cheeks, I thought what horrible rain it was. As I glanced toward the cemetery, a shiver wrenched my body and I broke out in gooseflesh. I could not stop shaking. Pale flames were weaving about in the air above the corpses, thrown up into the sky by the wind as if they were searching for the families they could no longer meet in life. I fled to the refuge of the tent, petrified, and threw myself down. When I was relieved from duty, I wrapped a blanket around my head and tried unsuccessfully to sleep. This was the worst experience I had during that time; even recalling it now, I shudder.

On the morning of August 15, the last day of the war, I left the headquarters to contact the army marine division in the Ujina district. On the way I passed a ruined house. In the garden I saw a white-faced youth sitting cross-legged by the water tap and a woman pouring water over his body. I stopped and asked the woman if he was her son. She replied that he was. "He said he was hot . . . he can't eat. I think he'll die soon," she said sadly. The youth's swollen face was smeared with white ointment; the darkened skin was peeling from his arms. He was listless and could not talk. He was just waiting for death, leaning against a shutter without moving. He was about my age. By pouring water over him, his mother was able to express her love for her doomed son.

As I was about to leave, I noticed a book with a bright red cover lying on the ground among several magazines. I picked it up and found it was an English translation of Soseki Natsume's *Botchan*. It was stained with rain. As I was flipping through the pages, I heard the woman call to me to keep it. I put it in my canvas bag and set off again for Ujina. I still have that book as a reminder of Hiroshima. Whenever I look at its red cover, the terrible scenes of that time spring to mind in kaleidoscopic fashion, wringing my heart.

At Ujina I found most of the buildings of the army marine division destroyed. Through a window I saw the commanding officer sitting at his desk in a room with no ceiling, holding his officer's sword in front of him and contemplating something. Just before lunch, I think, I heard the command for all personnel to gather around a radio. It was a broadcast by the Emperor, but I could not hear very well because of the static. Afterward we were told that the war was over. Some of the noncommissioned offi-

cers were crying uncontrollably, unable to believe that Japan
had lost. I, however, felt relief at the thought that now I could go
home to my mother rather than sorrow at Japan's defeat.

A few days later I left Hiroshima and headed back to my division in Tadanoumi. I was demobilized on September 5 and returned to my mother's home village on the Noto Peninsula in
Ishikawa Prefecture, where my family had been evacuated. A
roll of blankets and clothes on my back, I stood in the entrance of
my uncle's house and called out, "Hello!" My aunt, in the
kitchen area, stood up and called out my name. Hearing her
voice, my mother came running out barefoot, took my hands in
hers, and in a small voice said, "I thought you'd died in Hiroshima." Tears were flowing down her cheeks.

This ends the account of my experiences in Hiroshima. Compared with the suffering of those who were direct victims of the
bomb and those who lost their dear ones to it, my suffering was
infinitesimal. I have written of what was burned into the memory and chiseled in the body of a seventeen-year-old boy.

On August 6, 1977, thirty-two years later, I visited Hiroshima
again. The East Drill Ground where we had burned the bodies
was now a station for the San'yo Shinkansen "bullet train."
The rivers that had been filled with the injured and the dead
were now used for pleasure boating. In Peace Memorial Park,
where memorial services for the victims are held, young couples
who had never known war walked hand in hand. That, I
thought, is peace.

As long as we live, we must carry the cross of being victims of
the atomic bomb. We walk a path of thorns both physically and
mentally. I pray for the souls of the hundreds of thousands who
died in the vile bombing, call on governments to abolish nuclear
weapons, and encourage all the victims of the bomb to work together for enactment of a Hibakusha Aid Law to protect us.

The Longest Day

Hiroshi Sawachika

Doctor, please help my child.'' The words seemed to have been wrung out of the woman who had come bursting into the infirmary, her clothes in tatters. I was in the process of trying to extract hundreds of splinters of glass embedded in a boy's skin. I looked up from my labor to see the proffered child, who had already stopped breathing and lay limply in its mother's arms.

Taking a closer look at the woman, I realized that she had lost her sight, probably from the flash of the bomb. "It's all right now, we'll take care of your child for you. Don't worry anymore,'' I told her and, making a sign to the nurse, took the dead child from its mother's tight grasp and had it removed to another room. "Thank you, thank you, you've made it all worthwhile, coming all this way. Thank you.'' Her thanks died away, and she sank down in exhaustion.

No sooner had I treated one person than another arrived and sat dumbly before me. My tired hands moved mechanically as I continued working on the unending procession of people. "Doctor, milk's arrived.'' When the nurse gave me a cupful, I realized I had neither eaten nor drunk anything since morning, but I only became conscious of the pangs of hunger after swallowing the sweet, refreshing milk. The events of the day returned to my memory, juggling themselves like the pictures of a revolving lantern.

Always late setting out for work, on that particular day I had left my home in Kusatsu, four kilometers from the center of Hiroshima, thirty minutes early to go to work at the headquarters of the army marine division in the Ujina district. I was waiting for a streetcar in front of Koi Station, with about a hundred people lined up in front of me, when I noticed a sergeant who worked in the same office standing second or third from the front and beckoning me. I hurried up to him, and he let me into the line with him, whispering how glad he was to see me.

As I entered my office, I was aware that it was going to be another hot day. I was just sitting down when everything outside my window was stained red and I felt heat on my cheeks. My first thought was that an incendiary bomb had exploded, and I was running over to the window to look when I suddenly felt as if I had been caught up in a vacuum. When I regained my senses, both the frame and the glass of the window were gone, and my desk was lying in a heap as though it had been pushed from one side. Feeling dampness on my right cheek, I put up a hand to touch the place and found a small graze from which blood was flowing. I realized that my white shirt was soaked red. Investigating, I could find no particular injury. Thinking it strange, I turned to find that the office worker who had been beside me had sustained a severe injury and was losing a lot of blood. It was her blood that had soaked me. I shouted an order to evacuate the building and did my best to staunch the flow.

Waiting for the next attack, I became conscious of an oppressive stillness. Feeling detached from the events around me, I stood up and looked outside. A ball of fire was swirling into a cloud that rose skyward, eventually turning into a huge white mushroom shape. I watched, fascinated.

I was brought back to reality by the voices of nurses calling out to patients. A long, slow-moving line awaited the skillful but necessarily meager emergency treatment of the medical orderlies and nurses. I remember a young woman sitting in front of me, holding what appeared to be a red scarf against her neck with her right hand. I asked what was wrong, and she replied expressionlessly that she had been injured slightly on the right side of the neck. I saw then that the red cloth was a white handkerchief, stained and clotted with blood, stuck to her neck. I carefully eased the handkerchief away and to my horror saw that a wedge of white concrete had lodged itself deeply in her neck. As I probed, I watched the woman's face and asked if I was hurting her. She replied firmly that there was no pain. She told me that part of the building she had been working on had collapsed in fragments.

Her injury was far beyond my equipment or skill; all I could do was give her emergency treatment. I still feel my inadequacy, like a constantly borne cross. Her beautiful profile and transparently white face, as she nodded wordlessly and disappeared into the crowd, remain clear in my memory.

I became aware of a strange humming, as if of a multitude, pressing nearer. A horde of burned people was shuffling toward us. Some were in tatters; others had strips of skin hanging down from the arms they held out before them; still others, the gore of their wounds already dried on their clothing, could hardly walk. We were overwhelmed by this flood of people and, at a loss, hurried to open up the large assembly hall. We ordered drums of peanut oil to be taken from our stores and mixed the oil with talc to make an ointment whose use we quickly explained to our soldiers, who undertook the emergency treatment of the burned. In an instant the characteristic smell of grilled cuttlefish and cooking oil began to rise from every part of the hall.

Those who had received treatment changed places with those still waiting. So great were the numbers that a field hospital was set up under temporary roofing on the waterfront. There seemed no end to the numbers admitted because they could no longer stand. To meet the emergency, the headquarters staff mobilized the remaining vessels and inaugurated a transport service to aid stations and medical facilities on nearby islands. The bustle of activity rapidly filled the area.

Tired and needing to rest my hands, I walked out into the

grounds for a while. The brilliant sunlight was screened by the soot-laden smoke clouds rising in the northwest, and sultry heat wrapped my body. When I realized that the greater part of the city had been engulfed in flames, I began to wonder what kind of weapon could have caused such destruction with only a single flash and a dull explosion. It was beyond comprehension.

Something at my right foot was impeding movement. I looked down and saw that a young woman was clutching my leg tightly with both hands. "Doctor, I haven't a chance, but I know my baby is still alive in my stomach. Save it, please." For a moment no words came as I saw the flicker of hope in her tired eyes. "Very well, then," I answered with difficulty. "I'll get you to surgery. Be strong a little longer." I raced back to the clinic, where there had been no diminution in the number of patients awaiting treatment. There was no delivery room there, no equipment, no personnel, and above all, no time. My heart was torn by the difficult choice between the badly injured, many of them breathing their last, and the life of an unborn child. I still cannot keep myself from regretting that I was not able to fulfill that last, piercing plea of the dying mother-to-be.

The present intruded on my emotions. "Doctor, what do you think about this patient?" "Doctor, do something. It hurts." The hours slipped by. I gulped down a simple soldier's meal and felt my strength return. Then, as if compelled, I found myself drawn back to the pregnant woman. A chill wind blew through my heart as I looked down at her already cold body, and a feeling of emptiness filled me. I thought of my own pregnant wife, whom I had left at home that morning.

The fingers of fire seemed to be spreading more and more widely throughout the city. Though evening had fallen, the western sky was bright and reflected its light on the cheeks of the people. At our feet, already lost in darkness, the black shadows of the voiceless lay stretched out, on and on without end.

Born of the Bomb

Kayoko Satomi

There was a time when I was a tomboy, running about and never tiring of my games. I wonder where that child went. A day came when for some reason I tired easily, overcome by languor. The early summer sun seemed terribly bright to me. When I stood up from my desk, I felt dizzy and short of breath. My pulse rate shot up above a hundred. Resting on my bed, I saw, through the tears welling up uncontrollably in my eyes, some spots on my arm. My heart missed a beat as the thought "radiation sickness" assaulted me. No matter how I tried to exorcise the thought, it kept returning. The year was 1958 and I was thirteen. I felt acutely what it meant to be an atomic bomb survivor.

Another day, this one in the autumn of my eleventh year: underneath the high blue sky, hypnotizing and all-absorbing, I sat in a dim room in an old farmhouse, a post card in my hand. It advised me that as an atomic bomb victim I could have a free health checkup. I read and reread it, but I could not mistake my own name: Kayoko Mori. Arriving unexpectedly, the post card was a messenger of fear. Even now, that moment returns in my dreams. I was stunned and frightened. I knew that my family had been in Hiroshima when the bomb was dropped and that I had been in my mother's womb at the time. But I had never connected that fact with my own status as an atomic bomb victim until that day when I was eleven years old. I was convinced that I had radiation sickness and went for the medical examination in great trepidation. When I was given a clean bill of health, all my forebodings disappeared, and I returned to my afternoon classes in the highest of spirits.

Still another day impinges on my memory. I was five years old. It was the end of May, and the smell of new grass was rising all around. I was on my way with my sister Mitsuko to play on the river bank when a crowd of boys surrounded us. "Don't walk along the road in front of our house," they yelled. "We don't let atomic kids come around here. Atomic kids! Atomic kids!" Their taunts had Mitsuko in tears. I could say nothing coherent, could only spit out, "You're all stupid." A homemade knife grazed my sister's cheek and drew blood as it cut into my upper lip.

Yet another day, I do not remember exactly when, a woman and a little girl were stealing a look at my sister and me as they passed us in the street. "Look at that girl. Why is she like that?" "If you aren't a good girl, that's what will happen to you, too. So be sure to do what Mummy tells you." I do not think the words reached my sister's ears, because I was talking as fast as I could to cover them. Knowing Mitsuko's disfigurement to be keloids caused by the atomic bombing, I bit my lip to hold back my indignation and anger. I mustn't do anything to bring my sister any more pain, I told myself.

Such instances were not rare. There were even people who would stare openly at Mitsuko, with her limply hanging head, brazenly moving their eyes over her from head to foot. Many conversations like the one above did reach her ears. I would snuggle close to her, trying to take my share of her sadness, pain, and anger. I tried to draw those impudent stares to myself, too. I thought it was the only way to defy something unreasonable that hurt my sister excruciatingly.

August 6, 1945: my parents and sisters, Masako and Mitsuko, were living in Ushita, two and a half kilometers from the hypocenter. My brother and other sister had been evacuated and so escaped the disaster. In that hot Hiroshima August, under the wide blue sky, the city burned hotter than the sun itself and was made a melting pot by the bomb's explosion.

Masako, a first-year student in girls' secondary school, was out doing demolition work as a student-worker. She was on the site, we do not know exactly where, when the bomb fell. Mitsuko, then four years old, was on her way to play at a drill ground near our house. In the second that the flash sped like lightning through the city, her clothes caught fire, and by the time she had tumbled into the house, she was a mass of flame.

My father had already left for work. In the little time that he had to himself in the morning, he was smoking a cigarette. After the bomb fell, he regained consciousness to find himself walking along the road home. Columns of fire spouted here and there, and people were wandering around aimlessly like ghosts, or rather, monsters, screaming incomprehensible words. He said it reminded him of pictures of the lowest hell, whose inhabitants suffer interminable pain. After taking shelter in a drainage ditch from a shower of black rain, he finally made his way to our house by a roundabout route. It was evening by that time. His body was covered with blood, yet miraculously, he had few external injuries. His right arm was broken, and he had several unexplained scratches.

My mother had been inside the house. Fingers of devouring flame had crept to within two hundred meters, but luckily had not taken our house in their grip. However, fragments of shattered glass had embedded themselves all over my mother's body. Mitsuko was suffering from horrifying burns. The three of them waited outside on the nearby hillside for Masako to come home. The sun went down, ending a nightmarish day. The next morning, when it rose again to shine down on the charred earth of Hiroshima, Masako still had not returned.

My father spent the day walking through the streets of the city. The following day, my pregnant mother joined him in searching for my sister. Bodies were everywhere, black with flies. Corpses burned to sticks were piled in mounds. Through the reek of burned flesh my parents walked, day after day, gazing intently into the face of each corpse. They found nothing that they could identify as my sister and reluctantly left Hiroshima on August 11.

In his diary my father wrote, "I could have come across my daughter somewhere. Seeing the swollen, discolored bodies and faces changed beyond all recognition, it was very difficult to be sure if my daughter was among them."

After my parents returned to their home village of Tsutsuga in the mountains of Hiroshima Prefecture, my father collapsed with symptoms of radiation sickness and hovered near death. The blood flowing from his gums could not be stopped, all his hair fell out, and he became emaciated from running a high fever for more than a week. Those who came to visit him thought that he was in such bad condition that it would not be long before he was in the grave. But my father refused to give up. He would not die and leave his wife and children behind. He kept up his spirits by trying anything that he heard might be effective against his illness. He decocted a brew from the medicinal weed *dokudami;* he drank the blood of black carp; he ate a kind of green caterpillar that lives in trees. It seems like a miracle, but his temperature returned to normal in a month. However, it was three months before he could get around the room and a year before he returned to work, his broken arm mended and his illness abated.

Everyone had given up Mitsuko for dead, so bad were the burns that the bomb had inflicted. She had lost control of her neck muscles, so that her head bobbed around like that of a newborn baby. Her hair had fallen out, and maggots wriggled around beneath her burned flesh. My sister had no strength to do more than whimper for help. The autumn winds were blowing by the time all the maggots had been extracted, one by one, with tweezers. The helpless little four-year-old had been put through torture. It was probably because of my mother's devoted nursing that she pulled through. Wherever she had been burned, keloids remained.

My father's diary: "A cold December morning. My wife went

into labor. She gave birth to a girl. Fortunately mother and child are both well despite our fears that after the recent events that had taken such a toll on us the birth might not be easy and the child might not be all right. It is the only joyful thing that has happened to us this year. The villagers are all delighted, and we have named the child Kayoko, in the hope that she will live a fragrant life.'' And so I was born, my parents' fifth child, taking the place of my dead sister Masako, on December 9, 1945, in the village of Tsutsuga.

The nightmarish year finally drew to an end, and the new year began with renewed hope. But the imprint of the fiendish bomb did not disappear from our home. My mother, who had had virtually no injuries, fell sick, and the family had to be split up to allow her to fight the illness. A little over a year later, in 1950, after a brief respite a bout of pneumonia led to complications, and she was no more. I was four years old.

Until I was twelve I was brought up by my grandmother in Tsutsuga. I loved the changing seasons and the natural beauty around me, and played, brown and happy, a young girl full of dreams. Nothing troubled me very deeply, and I thought that the future was as open to me as the shining blue sky. Thus the post card was like a bolt from the blue. It was probably natural that when I was told there was nothing to worry about I felt triumphant and promptly forgot that I was a bomb victim.

I knew nothing of the war. I could not imagine how human beings could kill one another as if stamping on insects. How could I realize that the bomb had affected me? I had not even been born! Nevertheless, the radiation I had received in my mother's womb made me as much a victim as if I had been directly exposed. The symptoms that made themselves felt in the early summer when I was thirteen told me this in no uncertain terms. I wanted to escape. I wanted to reject the possibility of such a problem having anything to do with me. As if it were something I could rinse away with washing, I scrubbed at my skin with my tears, but the spots, as if deriding me, grew redder and redder.

On July 10 that year I received word that my grandmother

was critically ill. I had relied on her for support and had been yearning to bury my face in her breast and sob my heart out. The next day she died. I could not cry. All I could think was that I would soon be interred in the same grave. Then I heard my beloved grandmother's voice in the rhythms of village life: "Kayo, I haven't died. I haven't left you behind. Be strong. Live. As long as you live, I will live on with you." I stopped thinking of suicide, reassured by the thought that my grandmother was indeed the village itself. However, the future that had seemed so bright, the joyful life I had led, seemed to be buried with my grandmother. From that time on, I acknowledged myself to be a child of Hiroshima, actually born on August 6.

A shadow continued to lie on my heart. My knowledge of the nature of radiation sickness was rudimentary, so whenever I caught cold I shuddered with fear at the shadow of impending death. Although at that time I was a Christian and thought that in humanism could be found the greatest good, I would have preferred to die rather than live with my fears, and in dying curse those who waged war. I grew to hate all those adults, including my father, who had not opposed the war or who remembered it with nostalgia. I felt that I was tightly shackled, and when I began to think about what would happen to me in the future, I would hallucinate that I was falling in an endless spiral.

For a long time I lived with both love and hate for others warring in my heart. That I was eventually able to find my way out of the darkness was due to a revelation I received from the natural world, which I had loved since childhood. In nature animals and birds, trees and grass, were forced to suffer the cruelty of human beings, yet they were able to rise above their fate and survive. When I realized that, I felt that at last I had emerged from a bottomless bog.

However much I struggled, though, I could not throw off the burden of my birth as a victim of the bomb. I accepted the fact that I was an in utero victim and began to ask myself what kind of life I was going to lead knowing that. But ridicule awaited me:

"You didn't really experience the bomb." "You have no idea of the suffering." Or there was a kind of sympathy: "It would be better if you kept quiet." I paid no attention, letting such comments pass me by like the wind.

I believe that by being in my mother's womb I shared her suffering and saw with her the destruction of Hiroshima. Those experiences imbued me with sympathy for the weak and with hatred of injustice; I wanted to find meaning in life through considering the problems of people as a whole, not just my own problems.

As time went by, references to the atomic bomb began to disappear from school textbooks, and the postwar period came to an end. I was of an age to fall in love. But anyone who became friendly with me would hasten away as soon as I said I was an atomic bomb victim. From the time I was thirteen I thought that marriage, however happy a state, would never be for me. It saddened me beyond bearing that those with whom I formed a close relationship should treat our friendship as so much waste paper.

Then came a young man who extended his hand to me, who seemed to have some understanding of the bomb survivors' movement. He tried to make me forget that I myself was a victim. I did not doubt his love, and my feeling for him deepened. Eventually we received the permission of both our families to marry and visited each other's hometowns. Thus the happy days flew by.

At his parents' request, we postponed our wedding until after our graduation. Even then, however, the wedding date remained unfixed, since he had not obtained the teaching job that he had wanted. Then, five years after we had met, the blow fell. I should have known what would happen. I do not want to go into detail, but what he said to me when he broke the relationship pierced me, and the pain of the wound is still with me. "My father says he doesn't care who I marry as long as it isn't you. To tell the truth, my father and I both prefer not to have the blood of an atomic bomb victim in the family."

Whenever I was wounded because I was a survivor, I brooded about death. I told myself that death was the spring that lay at the end of my wintry road, and I prayed for its day to come. However, there beside me was my father, who at my entreaty broke a long silence to write down what had happened that day. And there was my sister, who did not try to hide her keloids. And there were the other survivors, who had patiently borne their burdens, urging on their aging bodies and supported by medication, many involving themselves in the movement to make the government acknowledge responsibility for the war and enact a Hibakusha Aid Law. And finally there were my pupils, deaf children undiscouraged by their handicap, living cheerfully and optimistically. How could I turn my back on all these people and render my life as an in utero victim completely meaningless?

Long ago, when I accused my father of being a willing accomplice to war, he said to me, "I was taught not to consider war a bad thing." I became a teacher of the deaf. It was through my contact with my pupils, friendly children far more cheerful than I had imagined, with their parents, some of whom who told me they had considered family suicide, and with deaf adults, whom I had come to know while learning sign language, that I gradually changed my vague ideas and way of looking at things. When I spoke of being a victim of the Hiroshima bombing at a meeting of deaf people, they said to me, "The handicapped loathe war. We're of no use to anybody in a war. We're not treated as human beings. A government that isn't concerned about the welfare of the handicapped could easily turn into a warmonger." These words reveal a clear understanding of the realities of the past as well as the present for the deaf.

I found that some of my teenage pupils were fascinated by the idea of war. Since they could not hear talk of war, their knowledge came from printed matter, and much of the fascination tended to be with tanks, fighter planes, and battleships, and with the sense of the victor's superiority. It was much more difficult to communicate the truth of war to these children than I had thought. I used what had happened to me to demonstrate to them the reality of war. As a teacher, I felt that the error of war could not be permitted to recur.

About thirty years after the war, the media started taking up the topic of in utero survivors. As a survivor and as one who earnestly desired true peace, I allowed myself to be exposed to the world's gaze, not considering whether I liked it or not. I became a minor celebrity in the school, and most of the children associated my name with Hiroshima and the atomic bomb. Some asked me to talk more about my experiences.

When a poem appeared in the book *Children of the Atomic Bomb,* I discovered a wonderful expression in sign language. The three words *peace, equality,* and *natural* are expressed by a single sign. In the long history of humankind, the deaf have received little education and have often been treated as no better than animals, yet in their language they have aptly expressed a truth. My discovery gave me great joy. Politics has always favored the strong; yet it is from among the crushed and oppressed that truth has emerged. I am convinced that the day will come when everyone will share their view.

Today I am married to a man who was able to accept me for what I was, and I am the mother of two children. Happiness had always slipped through my fingers, but now I have a warm family life and great contentment. Nevertheless, I cannot help feeling that the disease of the bomb is still lurking somewhere, sharpening its claws in readiness to pounce, and that the bomb's shadow of death may envelop my children. When I think of the possible effects on my children, I can hardly bear the pain. I talk to them of the beauty of life, lest a day come when they tell me they wish they had never been born. If such a time should come, I want to be able to say with conviction, ''I have fought for peace.''

My experience of the atomic bombing began in the postwar period, continues in the present, and will undoubtedly last until the day I die. The issue of the atomic bomb does not belong to history; it affects us here and now. The embodiment of the greatest crime in human history, what happened in Hiroshima and Nagasaki in August 1945 will remain with us until nuclear weapons are banned from the face of the earth.

Surely it is our duty as adults in the world today to communicate our experience of war and the atomic bombings, acting as a bridge to a time when peace and equality will be taken for granted; to find ways to build a society that will never need to send its children off to war; to battle daily with those who countenance war. I hope that I will never be asked by children in the future, as I asked my own father, why I never opposed war. And I hope that neither this country nor the world will ever again face destruction through the flames of war. It is up to each and every one of us to ensure that history does not repeat itself.

Traces of the Bomb

Michiko Fujioka

That morning at eight fifteen I was leaning against the wall of the factory, talking lightheartedly with my friends. I was wearing baggy work trousers made by my mother from an old indigo-and-white patterned kimono of hers, wooden clogs, a short-sleeved white uniform blouse, and a white headband inscribed with the word *patriotism*. Slung around my shoulders was my padded air-raid hood, made of the same material as my trousers; and stuffed in my satchel, made from my mother's sash padding, were a triangular bandage and some rice crackers. In a little while the bell for assembly would ring. Just as I was beginning to think I should make a move so as not to be late, a brilliant pale blue flash split the sky.

I was fifteen, in my third year at a girls' secondary school. I had last done any real studying in my second year. Now schoolwork was the last thing that concerned us; one day we were doing a ten-kilometer route march carrying ten-kilogram packs, another day worshiping at Gokoku Shrine, and another paying a study visit to the East Drill Ground. A week's volunteer labor at the army garment factory in the Ujina district followed.

The work at the garment factory was bitterly hard. Our job

182

was to unpack bloodstained army uniforms, so filthy that we could not see the texture of the material. We steeled ourselves against the bloody smell and the thick dust as we verified the original owner of the garment from the name tag. We unpacked the uniforms uncomfortably aware that the men who had worn them must be dead. But nobody voiced the thought.

Whenever I went to the factory and saw the huge mound of uniforms, I had an uneasy feeling that we were losing the war. But once I stepped out of the factory, my uneasiness evaporated as I heard martial music in the streets, listened to news of our victories, and watched the soldiers marching by, the sound of their boots reverberating. It was a marked contrast to the depressing atmosphere of the factory.

At that time I was never able to go to bed in my nightwear. Since my parents lived some distance away, I was boarding in Senda-machi to be near the school. When the air-raid sirens sounded, I would run to the shelter carrying a piece of matting from my room. The shelter, a trench dug in the garden of the boardinghouse, was always full of seepage. We would use the pieces of matting we had brought with us to cover the trench and then crouch down silently in the water until the all-clear. We often remained there, drenched to the waist, in silence for an hour. It was suffocating in that confined space, with ten or so of us packed together. If we raised the matting even slightly, the teacher in charge or the boardinghouse supervisor would scold us. After the all-clear we would throw ourselves down on the grass and, looking up into the sky, softly sing songs of the women's volunteer labor corps.

Strangely, I never thought that I was having a hard time of it. Perhaps it was because we had been taught that we were fighting a holy war and believed that we would win. When I heard that an American or British plane had been shot down, an enemy battleship sunk, or a large number of enemy soldiers killed, I clapped my hands and stamped my feet in joy. The Americans and British were devils, animals, not to be thought of as human at all. Only the Germans and Italians could be considered human; the Japanese, meanwhile, were the children of the gods. So we were taught, and so I believed. Those who raised doubts about what they were taught I considered unpatriotic.

Gradually the war grew more intense, and food supplies began to run short. It was my duty as a Japanese to be satisfied to lunch on a small dumpling made of soybeans from which the oil had been extracted and to have *suiton,* a thin soup with noodle scrapings, for dinner. A piece of dumpling made from rice bran and mugwort was a real treat.

At the beginning of my third year of secondary school, we were sent as student-workers to the Hiroshima aircraft factory. After three weeks of training, we were assigned our tasks. I worked in the machine section. I made cockpit parts, cutting out sheets of duralumin and making holes in them. No mistakes were tolerated. In a couple of days our small, white hands were chapped and oil-grimed. The inspection at the end of the day was frightening; any slip or substandard work resulted in a severe scolding.

One day a friend got her finger caught in a press, and it was ripped off at the joint. Disregarding me as I stood rigid in horror, she scooped up the finger, now a meter beyond her, and murmuring, "Poor thing," wrapped it in a handkerchief. Only then did she begin to cry. The teacher in charge came up and chided her: "Be strong, as a true daughter of Japan should be. There's no need to cry. Good heavens, it's a small thing compared with what soldiers have to go through." So that's what it means to be a true daughter of Japan, I thought to myself. I had no confidence that I would ever rate such an appellation.

It was soon after this incident that the skies of Hiroshima were rent by the atomic bomb. One moment I was leaning against the factory wall; the next I was buried under the fallen building. Somehow or other I crawled out, for when I came to my senses I found myself running through a cloud of dust to the air-raid trench. We were all running in utter silence, our hair dusty and disheveled and our torn trousers dragging on the ground.

I do not know how long I stayed in the trench. I heard a voice telling us to make for the hills, and we ran off in that direction.

When I was halfway up a hill, I looked down at the city and was astounded to see a sea of flame. Someone told me that the last battle for the Japanese main islands had begun. So Hiroshima had finally become a battleground! Telling myself to keep calm and act like a true daughter of Japan, I walked on. At the top of the hill a friend and I climbed a loquat tree and sat on a branch.

Suddenly I began to think of my mother, father, and sisters at home. Not knowing what to do, I started crying and could not stop. Tears streaming down my face, I plucked the loquats hanging on the branch one by one and ate them, thinking that they would give me strength to face the enemy. As I was eating, large drops of rain began to fall. Clinging to the branch, I waited for it to stop. But it rained harder and harder, rain mixed with black earth, something I had never seen before.

After the rain more people began showing up on the hill. Their faces were swollen, their eyes were streaming with a discharge, and gloves hung loosely from their fingertips. From their faces it was impossible to tell who was a man, who a woman; it was only by the sight of a breast exposed by ragged clothing that I knew a figure to be a woman. When I looked closely, I realized that what I had thought to be gloves was the skin of the arms. There was a person with one breast gouged out, blood streaming over the chest, and another with one eye hanging out. Everyone was very quiet. At some point the hill became pervaded by a strange, nauseating smell.

When evening fell, tents were pitched on the hillside among the loquat trees, and straw mats were spread out. An aid station had been set up. We were instructed that those who could should attend to the injured and those in pain should lie down. I went around tending the injured. Attempting to pull up someone who crouched motionlessly, I found that all I had in my hands was burned skin that had slid from the man's arms. Cries for water and cries of pain began to rise: "My body's burning!" "Put oil on the burns. Hurry!"

The cry for oil prompted me to set off for the ruined factory at full speed. I knew there was oil there. I had to bring that oil back, I thought, as I ran the kilometer or more to the factory.

There in a collapsed building I found a can of machine oil, and taking it, I returned to the hillside. I oiled the triangular bandage I was carrying and walked around smearing the oil on the burned bodies.

I had no time to wonder whether what I was doing was helping the injured. All I thought was that it was my duty to respond to the pleas of those whose skin had peeled right off their bodies. Before the night was through, fifteen or so people were dead. Some died calling out loudly for their mothers; others breathed their last reciting the Imperial Rescript to Soldiers and Sailors. Some begged their parents' pardon for dying first, and others requested that messages be taken to their families. Several people asked me to take such messages. Even though I knew I had no hope of delivering them, I promised to do so. It did not matter very much whom the message was for as long as relief could be granted by reassuring the sender.

I stayed at the aid station for three days and two nights. On the afternoon of August 8 one of the teachers came to the hill and told those of us who had somewhere to go to make our way there. "Term is over for the present. The school is burned down and the principal is dead. Later we'll get word to you at home about school." We were issued notices certifying that we were victims of the disaster.

It was about three o'clock in the afternoon when I set out alone and on foot for Hiroshima Station. I had only the clothes I stood in and was barefoot. I had crossed Koi Bridge and was walking in the area of Fukushima-cho when I was given a lift by a passing truck. In front of the still-burning station I got off and joined the line of people walking along the tracks. As I was walking along silently, a middle-aged woman called out to me from beside the tracks, "You can't go barefoot in this heat. Come here, I'll give you some sandals." I went to her house and put them on.

Yaga, the station after Hiroshima, was full of people with bandaged heads, arms in slings, and faces and chests painted white with ointment. Somehow I clambered through the window of a train heading for Miyoshi. There I spent the night, and the next day I arrived home to a joyful welcome. I was there when the war ended.

When we heard the Emperor's broadcast on August 15, my father and I wept. But I was not sad. All I was concerned about was fleeing from the American soldiers. From the day of our defeat, my father spent his time laboriously making straw sandals on the assumption that if each member of the family had ten pairs we could walk a long way.

Seven years passed. I spent my young adulthood in poverty. All thoughts of the atomic bombing and the lost war disappeared from my mind. We had a hard time economically, and goods were very scarce, but at night I could sleep in peace, and I did not have to fear the sound of sirens. It was also nice to be able to think freely. I really thought the war was over and peace had arrived.

However, the war was not over in my body. The day I realized that was more than seven years after the surrender, when I had married and just given birth to my first child. Until that day, I had forgotten the war.

On the evening of the sixth day after his birth, my baby suddenly began to run a fever. His temperature was forty-two degrees Celsius and he would not drink. I immediately called the doctor and had an injection given. But blood began to well out of the spot where the needle had punctured the skin and would not stop. His temperature refused to go down. In addition, purple spots appeared on the backs of his hands and on his insteps. From the recesses of my memory I recalled that when the victims of the bomb were dying in pain, their symptoms had been spots, fever, and the vomiting of blood.

My son had been born on June 10, and his fever continued to run between forty and forty-two degrees until December 13. He also continued to vomit blood and to hemorrhage. As autumn deepened, he lost the ability to regulate his body heat. If I inadvertently let the room temperature drop, his body temperature would fall below thirty-six degrees and he would have difficulty breathing. All the doctors gave up hope. My husband, sister-in-law, and I maintained a constant watch, filling the room with steam to keep the room temperature at twenty degrees.

On December 13 his temperature fell and he was able to regulate his own body heat. However, by that time he was deaf and blind, could not suck or grasp, and had to have his bowels evacuated by enema.

The next year, when he could be taken out, I took him to the largest and best hospitals and clinics to have him examined. After a ten-day hospitalization, when various tests were carried out, I was told that he was irreparably impaired and did not have long to live. "Take care of him," the doctors urged me. Although I mentioned that I was a victim of the atomic bombing and that the symptoms were very similar to those of radiation disease, the more prestigious the hospital was, the more it rejected the possibility and told me not to jump to conclusions.

I was sorry for my child, who had such a short life before him, and took him everywhere with me. One day a relative called on me. "No one has ever given birth to an abnormal child in this family before. It's an embarrassment for us all to have you taking the baby around as you do. Please try to put yourself in our place," she said. A little while after that another relative mentioned that she had heard it cost a lot to support a handicapped person and said that it was a disgrace to the family. Thinking that dying with my infant in my arms was far preferable to living with such persecution, I started to leave the house, but my husband discovered me and stopped me.

Over and over again I thought, If only I were not a victim of the atomic bomb. I cursed the war. Nobody would admit that the bomb was the cause of my baby's problems. But I knew. If I had not been caught in the bombing, I thought, crying, I would not know such pain.

In the autumn of my son's second year, he died of pneumonia. For the two years that he lived, he never once smiled, made a sound, or expressed any needs. As I buried him I vowed never again to bring a child into the world.

Three years later, however, I became pregnant again. When my pregnancy was confirmed, I seriously considered terminat-

ing it. I thought that I had no right to have another child. I spoke
at length with my husband about what was best for us to do.
We decided it was no good trying to escape reality. If the baby
was like my first child, then it was our duty to bear with it as a
legacy of the terror of war. Even if we decided to go ahead with
an abortion, traces of the war would not be extinguished from
the world, from humankind, from the Japanese people. Another
factor in our decision to steel ourselves and go ahead with the
pregnancy was the duty to keep alive the horror of the atomic
bomb.

Our trepidation while waiting for the birth was beyond description, and those around us opposed our decision. The
daughter that was born to us was prone to fever, and until she
entered primary school her nursemaid took her to the doctor
every day. After she started school, she often had to be hospitalized and spent many days at home in bed.

When people asked me why my daughter was so weak, I in-
variably replied, ''I was a victim of Hiroshima; I think that's the
reason. My son died from something very like radiation sickness.'' I received varied reactions. I spoke that way because I
wanted people to know that the atomic bomb continued to
threaten the welfare of our family, not because I wanted sympathy.

My daughter eventually graduated from university and went
to work for a trading company. One morning when she was preparing to go to work, I noticed that her hair had fallen out in
places, leaving bald spots. I felt a tightness grip my chest. After
that she pinned hair over the bald spots as best she could. Two or
three months later she began complaining of a slight fever. Her
blood pressure rose to 170, and she had to rest two or three times
when climbing the stairs at home. Just at that time we got word
that checkups were being offered to second-generation bomb
victims, and we promptly applied. Results of the examination
carried out at the university hospital revealed a hormonal im-
balance, and our daughter was told she needed to have more in-
tensive thyroid tests.

In time my daughter married and gave birth to a girl, who was born prematurely and spent the beginning of her life in an incubator. My daughter and granddaughter still have to visit the hospital regularly.

Even now, so many years after the bombing, the disquiet it causes within me continues; it will remain with me as long as I live. And even after I die, traces of the war will continue to exist within my daughter and my grandchild. The other day, the flame from the Peace Tower in Hiroshima passed through my town. I accompanied it for four kilometers on my motor scooter as an expression of my conviction that, however humbly, I have to take a stand against nuclear war.

The Turning Point

Akihiro Takahashi

I have never forgotten that day. Rather, I cannot forget it. I have heard that the brain has a mechanism to suppress traumatic memories. I have not let that happen. I have disciplined myself not to forget, however painful it may be to remember, for that day was the turning point of my life.

The sky was blue and clear. The boy I was then, looking up into the sky, was an ordinary child of a nation at war, a second-year student at the Hiroshima Municipal Middle School. As I was to find out later, Japan's hopes for victory had faded, and the war by then was almost lost. Such a situation was incomprehensible to a boy just turned fourteen. I had grown up in Hiroshima, which had been a city of the military since the Sino-Japanese War in the late nineteenth century, and like my classmates I looked up to soldiers and hoped to emulate them. I thought of the young naval air cadets at the school in Kasumigaura, Ibaraki Prefecture, with their white uniforms and caps and their short swords. Ah, that's what I want to be when I finish school, I thought.

August 6, 1945. I had a cold and had had a headache since waking up. I was ashamed to miss school for such a slight ailment, though, and, befitting a boy whose country was at war, I set off stalwartly for school, saying nothing to my parents. We had been mobilized as student-workers and sent out to munitions factories, demolition sites, and farming villages to contribute our labor. We were then doing demolition work in the Koami-cho district, but that day the first-year and second-year students, 147 boys in all, were spending a rare day taking regular classes at school.

At eight o'clock we had all arrived and were in the schoolyard waiting for the call to assembly. Our eyes were fixed on the door to the staff room as we watched for the teachers to appear. Then one of my classmates pointed to a patch of sky, calling out, "Look! A B-29!" I shifted my gaze and saw a B-29 flying overhead. By that time one or two planes did not rate an air-raid warning, let alone an air-defense alarm, the appearance of B-29s having become a daily event.

The B-29, trailing a stream of vapor, floated in the sky above us. The class captains shouted for us to fall in. We formed ordered ranks and turned our eyes toward the door again. Two or three teachers appeared in the doorway and started to walk out. At that instant there was a sound like a roar, and everything around me turned pitch black. When I opened my eyes, I was enveloped in a dense brown cloud of smoke.

I had been blown about ten meters from where I had been standing. Then I realized I had been standing still for quite a while, watching the smoke. What happened? I asked myself in bewilderment. I could not understand the situation, and in confusion I threw myself back down on the ground.

I do not know how much time passed. Five minutes, maybe ten. Finally the smoke thinned, and I began to pick out features in the schoolyard. Here and there classmates were lying. The school building had collapsed. And not only the school building; every building in the vicinity had disappeared.

For a moment I thought that Hiroshima had vanished. Then I told myself it must have been a bomb. I decided to set off in the direction of the river, remembering that we had been repeatedly told during evacuation drills to take refuge there if a bomb fell. Near the school ran the Yamate River. I decided to go there.

When I made a move, I caught sight of myself and felt a stab of shock. The palms of my hands were swollen like blowfish and blistered. The exposed skin was yellow, and the skin of both arms and legs had peeled and was hanging down like flapping rags. My uniform had been burned to tatters, and one of my puttees had gone. My back was burning hot. Frantically I ran from the schoolyard into the street.

"Takahashi! Takahashi!" A voice was calling my name. Looking around, I saw a classmate, Tatsuya Yamamoto, who lived in Kusatsu, like me. His skin, too, was hanging in shreds. All the hair that had not been hidden under his forage cap had been burned off. I put my hand up to my head, and sure enough, I found that I had no hair, either. Suddenly I was overpowered by dread.

Tatsuya, who was gazing around vacantly, began murmuring, "I wonder if my house has burned down." I made no reply, but he continued, "What will we do if our parents have been killed?"

We made our way to the river, walking through a scene out of hell. I saw a middle-aged man still managing to walk although the skin of the upper half of his body had been completely burned away, exposing the flesh beneath; a man with slivers of glass embedded in his chest; a woman with an eyeball dangling on her cheek; a baby wailing beside its mother, who had been burned to a charred lump, her hair blown completely opposite to its natural fall; corpses with their entrails tumbling out; a horse, only raw flesh, lying dead with its head in a cistern. Tatsuya began crying for his mother. I had a stronger hold on myself, and I scolded him and told him to stop crying.

All the lanes were blocked by the debris of collapsed houses, over which we crawled. Glass and nails cut into our arms and legs. At last we reached the river bank, which was also covered with broken glass and rubble. Our arms and legs were a mass of cuts and bruises, though strangely enough we felt no pain. Spanning the river was a wooden bridge just wide enough for two people. Still more or less crawling, I began to cross.

When I had gone a little way, I heard a roaring sound. Looking around, I saw the whole area I had just come through in the grasp of flames four to five meters high, which were devouring the collapsed houses. The brilliant red of the blaze burned into my eyes. That was close! I thought. If I'd been only a few minutes later . . . I burst into tears and then found I could not stop crying. I looked around to see what had happened to Tatsuya but could see no trace of him. Much later his mother told me that someone had taken him up on the back of a bicycle and that he had died on September 16 that year. She said that before he died his belly turned purple and he vomited up a continuous stream of some blue-gray substance. His teeth loosened, and blood-flecked pus dribbled from his mouth and ears. His whole body was infested with maggots. He had had a massive dose of radiation and died a wretched death.

I crossed the bridge alone and reached the Yamate-cho bank. Then I sat down on a sandbank in the river. My back was burning unbearably. Unable to stand the pain, I ran into the river. The cool water was a blessing to my fevered body. Only when I was in the water could I forget the agony. Then I returned to the sandbank and rested. When I felt hot again, I immersed myself in the water. The gravel of the riverbed ate into the raw flesh of my arms and legs and made them hurt, but that was easier to bear than the burning of my back.

Corpses were floating down the river on the current. They flowed by me as I lay in the water.

Others were cooling themselves in the river. I saw one person lean forward to drink, his face in the water. At some point his body was taken up by the river and began floating away. It took me some time to realize that he had died where he was.

A middle-aged woman came up to me as I lay on the sandbank and exclaimed at how badly burned I was. She dabbed my body with an oily substance and told me to go to the aid station that had been set up in the Mitaki district by a team from a military hospital.

Enduring the burning pain, I set out. The tent that housed the aid station was filled with the moaning of women and children burned far worse than I was. Since my injuries were relatively light, the nurse merely swabbed my burns with an antiseptic. I rested for a while in the tent. It began to rain. I had never seen black rain before. The rain pattered down in large drops. The noise of the rain and the noise of the moaning inside the tent reverberated, filling me with dread. Is there really such a thing as black rain? I asked myself. Here was another thing I could not understand.

When the rain stopped, I slipped out of the tent and walked along the railway tracks of the San'yo Line. It normally took about an hour and a half to walk from Mitaki to Kusatsu. I thought that once I reached home, the pain and suffering would go away. The pain had seeped through my whole body, but I was still quite conscious. My remaining puttee had begun to get in the way, so I took it off and threw it away. As I was picking my way over fallen people, I heard my name called. It was a fellow student, Tokujiro Hatta, who also lived in Kusatsu.

"What's the matter?"

"I can't walk. Please help me."

"Why can't you walk?"

Tokujiro showed me the soles of his feet. The skin had been completely burned away, and the raw flesh was showing. There was no way he could walk like that. I thought he had done wonders to get this far and considered the best way to help him.

"Your hands haven't been hurt—try crawling on all fours," I suggested. He put his hands and knees on the ground. Slowly he crawled forward. After he had progressed a while in this manner, I pulled him upright, balancing him on his heels, and walked him along with his body leaning against mine for support. We both soon tired, however, and he went down on all fours again. And so we went on, alternately crawling and walking, helping each other.

"Please help me get home." He was groaning. We sat and rested when we were too tired to go any farther. I happened to be glancing at the other people going along the road when I saw my great-aunt and great-uncle walking toward us. They had been traveling to a memorial service for a relative in the country when they heard that Hiroshima had been destroyed. They were on

their way back to Kusatsu. I called out to my great-uncle as
loudly as I could. He was deaf and strode past me briskly. My
great-aunt, coming up behind, finally noticed me and hastily ran
to my great-uncle to bring him to a halt. I was put on his back,
and she and another relative with them helped Tokujiro. A little
while later a neighbor from Kusatsu passed on a bicycle, and
they asked him to tell our family to come at once with stretchers.
My great-uncle was well over sixty, and carrying my weight
could not have been easy.

I was ravenously hungry. I gulped down the two balls of white
rice that my great-aunt happened to have with her. It had been
years since I had eaten white rice, and it was unbelievably delicious. Tokujiro, though, ate nothing at all. They said later that
he died soon after reaching home.

In the vicinity of Koi we met my grandfather and some
neighbors carrying stretchers. They loaded us onto the stretchers, took us to the aid station at the Kusatsu Primary School
for treatment, then carried us home. I badly wanted a drink of
water, but my grandfather told me, "You shouldn't drink anything. They say everyone who's had water has died. Try to go
without." He refused to give me any.

My mother, having already prepared my bed, was waiting for
me. She told me later that when she saw my burns she almost
fainted. She cut off my clothes with scissors, wrapped me in a
brand-new gown, and put me to bed. It was then that I lost consciousness. They tell me that I became delirious from fever and
kept spitting out abuse of America. The hate must have been
lurking in my subconscious mind.

For the next three weeks I remained unconscious. My grandfather brought Dr. Hayashi, the ear, nose, and throat specialist
that we three children always went to, to the house to look at
me. It was said that the doctors of Hiroshima had been virtually wiped out. Just to find a doctor was a matter for rejoicing.
Dr. Hayashi continued to treat me every morning and evening.

I approached death a number of times. My family were told
by the doctor to resign themselves to losing me. My two younger
brothers, who had been evacuated to Miyoshi, were summoned

back home for a time, since my mother and grandfather wanted them to see me again before I died.

The days passed, and still I could not move from my bed. They were days of suffering. It was painful enough to have to lie staring up at the ceiling, unable to make the slightest movement, but having my injuries tended was even worse. Pus was oozing from my wounds, and at one stage maggots were breeding in my left leg. The gauze bandages were changed twice a day because of the pus that collected. I could see the blood and pus gush out when the doctor peeled the gauze away.

Having the gauze bandages changed was excruciatingly painful. "Stop it," I would scream, "you're hurting me. Damn you, stop it!" This would happen twice a day. My grandfather, mother, and neighbors would have to hold me down, pinning my arms and legs so I could not move. When my back was being attended to, I would heave around so much that it took the strength of several adults to keep me still.

At that time it was impossible to buy bandages. My grandfather would take the stained pieces of gauze down to the river and wash them, then boil them so they could be used again. He often took fresh fish, cigarettes, or one of my mother's kimono into the countryside to barter for food. It was a time when money was useless. The rice and fresh vegetables he brought back in exchange were to build me up.

My grandfather had lived many years in Hawaii and had done business there, so his English was reasonably good. British and Australian soldiers, part of the army of occupation, would often pass our house on their way to Miyajima and Iwakuni. He would stop them and tell them that I was a bomb victim and bedridden, and they would give him chocolate and other things. Once five or six soldiers came in to see me. My grandfather exclaimed angrily that America had inflicted terrible burns on even an innocent child. The soldiers' faces crumpled, and they murmured that they were sorry.

As I was lying in bed, I picked up many things indirectly from the talk around me. The bomb had been a new kind of weapon and had been dropped on Nagasaki as well as Hiroshima. In

Hiroshima alone, hundreds of thousands of people had been killed. Hearing that the war had been caused by the tyranny of the military was almost too great a shock to the fourteen-year-old I was then. I hate Hideki Tojo, I thought for the first time.

Other things that my family and neighbors whispered about came to my ears. People who had lived near us had died. Classmates had died. My best friend, Takashi Yamazaki, had died. Though my family never intended me to learn of these things, the news seemed to seep through to me. It was then that I began to fear that I too would die.

In the spring of 1946, just before I was able to leave my bed, Dr. Ishibashi, who had taken over my treatment from Dr. Hayashi, declared that I was out of danger. Those decisive words released me at last from the threat of death. The burns I had received had not yet healed completely, but they had stopped oozing pus. I began to get up and practice walking around the house with the aid of a stick. I wanted to see what it was like outside. As I was hobbling around the yard with my stick, the neighbors told me, "You were lucky to survive. It must have been terrible. But you'll be all right now." Some of them even wept, they were so happy to see me recovering. Many of them had lost friends and relatives to the bomb.

Tears flowed down the cheeks of the mothers of Takashi and Tatsuya. They said I had done well to come through all this and that it wouldn't have mattered if their own children had been left cripples if only they had lived. I felt these words the most keenly of all.

A year and a half after the bomb, in April 1947, I returned to school. Of the sixty boys in my class, only ten of us had survived.

Four fingers of my right hand, which had been very badly burned, were crippled and would not move, and my right elbow was frozen at a 120-degree angle. I tired easily and would sometimes be overcome by fatigue. The wounds I had received did not heal well, and my nose bled if I stayed out in the sun. I also came down with asthma attacks. I had no inkling that these could be aftereffects of the bomb.

On graduation from school, I wanted to work in an advertising company. But after the second interview, when even the salary and working conditions had been agreed upon, I received a letter of refusal from the company. They gave as their reason the fact that I could not ride a bicycle because of the damage the bomb had done to my hand. This was a bitter shock to me. The grim reality of being a victim of the bomb remained at the center of my consciousness from that time on.

I got a job at the Hiroshima city office through a friend's introduction. I was forced to realize that the way society looked upon me was quite different from the attitude of my fellow students. Whenever I rode a bus or streetcar or walked along the street, I found myself the object of stares. I grew ashamed of my keloids when people started staring and whispering. It became my custom to bandage the visible scars before setting off for work in the morning. If I rode on public transport, I stayed near the door. I fell into the habit of standing in corners. At meetings I tried to seat myself where no one could see me.

Sometimes strangers would speak to me as I was on my way to work. "Where were you when the bomb fell?" they might ask, or they would encourage me with the words, "Do your best despite your handicap." Most of those people either had lost loved ones to the bomb or had themselves been injured. I felt that only such people could understand what I was suffering.

Then, just as I was growing increasingly depressed about my situation, something happened in the Public Registration Section of the city office, where I was working at the time. We were all spring-cleaning the office. Despite my bad hand, I was helping the others move desks and chairs. Then one of my fellow workers snapped at me, "You're worse than useless. Go over there out of the way!" It was a great shock. After that I was all the more convinced that no healthy person could understand what it was like to be a bomb survivor.

About that time I read in the newspaper about the formation of a group for bomb survivors. It was a place for people who shared the same fate to confide their worries to one another and alleviate their mental pain. With my strengthened feeling that only survivors could understand survivors, I immediately became a member. However, as membership increased, some people began saying that the group should not be just a mutual-comfort society. Some members said we should compile accounts of our experiences of the bomb and urge the authorities to preserve the Atomic Bomb Dome—the prewar Industrial Promotion Hall, located near the hypocenter. Thus the group became more outward looking and urged that free medical treatment be made available to survivors and that facts concerning the bomb and the suffering it had caused be publicized. Despite my self-consiousness, I collected signatures in the street for the preservation of the Atomic Bomb Dome. That was the beginning of my work for the bomb survivors.

In 1953, on my doctor's recommendation, I had surgery on the keloids of my right hand. When the bandages were removed a month later, I found that I could hold a pencil and write much more easily than before. It was a small but joyful milestone. Little by little, my self-confidence was returning.

The following year I represented the bomb survivors at the Hiroshima Citizens' Conference Against Atomic and Hydrogen Bombs and was given the opportunity to speak of my experiences before more than a thousand Hiroshima residents. Despite my nervousness, I spoke of what had happened just as I have written it here. From the body of the hall I could hear the sound of sobbing. I had never thought that what I had to say would bring tears from my listeners. I felt at a loss amid the thunderous applause that I received, but at the same time I resolved that our experiences as bomb victims must become the kernel of a campaign against the spread of nuclear weapons.

I moved slowly toward participation in the antinuclear movement. After I had spoken at the conference, I became a spokesman for the victims more and more often and was drawn increasingly into the limelight. Shy by nature, I acted as advocate for the survivors while continuing to fight my embarrassment and nervousness. But I also came to believe that I had to speak on behalf of those who had suffered far worse than I had. When it was decided at a meeting of Hiroshima survivors that we would lobby members of parliament for the enactment of a

Hibakusha Aid Law, I was appointed to a group that would visit Tokyo once a year to petition legislators.

In 1957 I was elected an officer of the Japan Confederation of A- and H-Bomb Sufferers Organizations, formed the previous year. I became increasingly involved in the two issues supported by the confederation, enactment of a Hibakusha Aid Law and opposition to atomic and hydrogen bombs. However, to the disappointment of bomb survivors, the antinuclear movement in Japan was rent by ideological differences. At the first world conference, held in Hiroshima in 1955, participants from eleven countries had resolved that the tragedy of Hiroshima and Nagasaki should never recur. Successive conferences, however, became forums for publicizing political ideologies and party platforms.

I want to urge political parties who use the antinuclear movement for their own ends to stand back from the forefront of the movement. It is neither a political activists' antiestablishment movement nor a revolutionary movement. Rather, it is an anti-authoritarian movement opposing the dangerous syndrome that the possession of nuclear weapons engenders. It is necessary above all to continue our tenacious opposition to all nations that continue to test nuclear weapons and menace others through military power.

I married in 1961, at the age of thirty. My wife is not a survivor, but she has a deep understanding of survivors. There were survivors among her relatives and dearest friends. She is a woman who associated with survivors at a time when prejudice and discrimination ran deep.

My marriage was a great relief to my mother. My father had died of tuberculosis in 1944. After the war my mother made ends meet by working as a school cafeteria helper and as a seamstress. She could not afford to rest, what with my medical expenses and the treatment of my younger brother's tuberculosis. When I think of how the strength of my mother and my wife has enabled me to continue to function in society, I realize just how important sympathy and warmth from the people around them are to survivors. Because I came to understand the importance of the warmhearted support of relatives and friends, I decided to give more and more of my support to the activities of the confederation and began to deal with the issue of raising the living standards of survivors.

At that time I was working at the Hiroshima Peace Memorial Museum. The museum displays photographs showing what happened after the bomb fell, clothing worn by students, and roof tiles and everyday articles that were exposed to radiation. Once or twice a week I made the rounds of the museum as night watch. As I gazed at those reminders of the bombing in the still of the night, I recalled vividly the cruelty of the attack, and, being alone, I felt an inexpressible fear. My nervousness gradually became a neurosis. I decided to speak to my superior about my state of mind and in a short while was transferred to the Publicity Section.

My days continued to be busy, with my work for the city office and my duties as an officer of the confederation. I frequently worked all day Saturday and Sunday to get out the city gazette. I also had to meet with the reporters covering city hall and spent many late nights with them. As a result, fatigue began to accumulate, and in the spring of 1971, after a lobbying session for the confederation, I was hospitalized with chronic hepatitis. The damage to my liver qualified me for the first time to be registered as a victim of the bomb, so I was able to receive medical coverage under the Atomic Bomb Medical Treatment Law. Since then I have continued to suffer from hepatitis and other illnesses contracted as a result of the aftereffects of the bomb and have been in and out of hospital a number of times. Worry about my health has frequently made me wonder why it is necessary to go on living with such pain. At such times my wife's encouragement and the thought that I cannot render worthless the deaths of my friends killed by the bomb give me the strength to continue. I tell myself it is the mission of those of us who survived to transmit to succeeding generations the voices of those who died.

In 1979 I was appointed the sixth director of the Hiroshima Peace Memorial Museum. As part of my work I talked about my experiences to students from all over the country who visited the museum on school excursions, striving to convey the sufferings of the bomb victims.

In June 1980 I went to the United States with an exhibition of photographs and objects from Hiroshima and Nagasaki, which was shown to senators in Washington, D.C. At that time I had the opportunity of meeting retired Air Force Brigadier General Paul W. Tibbets, the pilot of the *Enola Gay,* the B-29 that dropped the bomb on Hiroshima. I had heard that four years previously, in 1976, General Tibbets had dropped a mock atomic bomb at an air show in Texas. I had felt at the time that his rash action disregarded those who hoped for a ban on nuclear weapons and that all our efforts were in vain.

I hear that General Tibbets hesitated before agreeing to meet me. However, when a reporter from the Chugoku Broadcasting Corporation spoke to me, I willingly agreed to the meeting. General Tibbets awaited me on a footpath skirting the park behind the building where our exhibition was being held. He was a fine-looking, bespectacled old gentleman, wearing a chocolate brown suit and carrying a briefcase of the same color. Our interpreter, Tadatoshi Akiba, an associate professor at Tufts University in Boston, introduced us. I extended my right hand, covered with keloids. "Was that from the bomb?" General Tibbets asked. "Yes," I replied. His face twitched.

I bridged the gap. "I don't want to bring up grievances here," I said. "You acted according to your orders. The problem lies with those who gave the orders. We survivors of the bomb, quite frankly, hate both the leaders of Japan who started the war and the American leaders who ordered the bomb dropped. But I think as human beings we have to go beyond hate. Only by going beyond all hate, all pain, and all sadness can we arrive at true peace."

"I understand how you feel." General Tibbets nodded. "That day the sky was blue, just as it is now in Washington."

"Yes, it was very clear. I saw your B-29 up in the sky."

"How old were you then?"

"Fourteen. I was in the second year of middle school."

Then I said, "Today just pressing a button will destroy

everything. That is why the atomic bomb survivors want complete nuclear disarmament.'' General Tibbets replied, ''If there were another war, I'd do the same thing again if I were ordered. That's the logic of war. That's why it's important not to allow war to occur.''

General Tibbets continued to grasp my right hand between his hands. There was something shining in his eyes. I suggested that we exchange addresses and correspond. General Tibbets took from his briefcase the embossed business card of the president of an air charter company and handed it to me. At last there was a smile on his face. When hate can be overcome, sympathy and trust can thrive on a human level. I still correspond with General Tibbets.

Hiroshima is not simply a fact of history. It is a warning and an admonition to the present, when the danger of nuclear war dominates everything. Some say that we are now only three minutes from nuclear conflict. We have to ensure that the hands approaching midnight on the clock are put back by five minutes, ten minutes—no, rather, we must prevent nuclear war.

The way to the abolition of nuclear weapons is long and steep. This means that we must speak out all the more loudly and put all the more strength into our efforts. The strength of one person is slight, perhaps, but no one is completely powerless. It is my conviction that peace will be built through the efforts of individuals. It is now that the strength of the individual is needed. From one person to two, from two to three, from three to four: with perseverance, slowly but surely the ring of peace will be widened.

Acknowledgments

O f the twenty-five essays in this book, all but those by Fumiko Harada and Akihiro Takahashi first appeared in English in somewhat different form in the monthly magazine *Dharma World* between January 1984 and January 1986. A portion of the essay by Akihiro Takahashi and the twenty-four other essays in their entirety were originally published in Japanese, as listed below, and are published in English with the permission of the authors and the original publishers.

Hiroshi Sawachika: *Gembaku Nikki* [Diaries of the Atomic Bombing], vol. 2. Edited and published by the Hiroshima Prefectural Medical Association, Hiroshima, 1970.

Akihiro Takahashi: Akihiro Takahashi, *Hiroshima—Hitori kara no Shuppatsu* [Hiroshima: Starting Out Alone]. Tokyo, Chikuma Shobo, 1978.

Kosaku Okabe, Hiroshi Shibayama, Teiichi Teramura, and Katsuyoshi Yoshimura: *Gembaku Hibaku Taikenki* [Personal Accounts by Atomic Bomb Victims]. Edited and published by the Kyoto Prefectural Association of Atomic Bomb Sufferers, Kyoto, 1979.

Lee Gi-sang and Sumiteru Taniguchi: *Nagasaki no Shogen* [Testimony from Nagasaki]. Edited by Sadao Kamata and published by Aoki Shoten, Tokyo, 1979.

Michiko Fujioka and Kayoko Satomi: *Jinrui no Mirai e no Shogen* [Witness to the Future of Humankind]. Edited by the National Association of Teachers Who Suffered Atomic Bombing and published by Rodo Jumposha, Tokyo, 1980.

Tadaomi Furuishi: *Kinoko-gumo wa Kietemo* [Though the Mushroom

Cloud May Disappear]. Edited and published by the Kobe Association of Atomic Bomb Sufferers, Kobe, 1980.

Fumiko Harada: *Hiroshima no Asa, soshite Ima* [That Morning in Hiroshima—and Today]. Edited by Junko Inazawa and published by Ayumi Shuppan, Tokyo, 1982.

Katsuo Fukushima, Sakae Hosaka, Masae Kawai, Machiyo Kurokawa, Asae Miyakoshi, Akira Nagasaka, Nakaichi Nakamura, Fumiko Nonaka, Misue Sagami, and Kiyoko Sato: *Gembaku o Sabaku* [The Atomic Bomb on Trial]. Edited by the Tokyo Council of A-Bomb Sufferers Associations and published by the Labor Education Center, Tokyo, 1983.

Shige Hiratsuka and Sachiko Masaki: *Heiwa o Negatte* [In Hope of Peace]. Edited and published by the Miyagi Prefectural Association of Atomic Bomb Sufferers, Sendai, 1984.

Sumiko Umehara: *Shogenshu Kanagawa* [Testimony from Kanagawa], vol. 1. Edited and published by the Kanagawa Prefectural Association of Atomic Bomb Sufferers, Yokohama, 1984.

Portions of the poem "America, Do Not Perish at Your Own Hands: In Protest of the Texas Air Show" by Sadako Kurihara are published with the permission of the Hiroshima/Nagasaki Memorial Collection of the Wilmington College Peace Resource Center, Wilmington, Ohio.

All photographs are used with the permission of the copyright holders. Credits for the photographs of Hiroshima and Nagasaki in 1945 are included in the captions. The seventeen photographs of survivors in recent years were taken by Ittetsu Morishita.